Colloquial
Cambodian

The Colloquial Series

The following languages are available in the Colloquial series:

Albanian
Amharic
Arabic (Levantine)
Arabic of Egypt
Arabic of the Gulf and
   Saudi Arabia
Bulgarian
Cambodian
Cantonese
Chinese
Czech
Danish
Dutch
English
Estonian
French
German
* Greek
Gujarati
Hindi
Hungarian
Indonesian

Italian
Japanese
Korean
Malay
Norwegian
Panjabi
Persian
Polish
Portuguese
Romanian
* Russian
Serbo-Croat
Slovene
Somali
* Spanish
Spanish of Latin America
Swedish
Thai
Turkish
Ukrainian
Vietnamese
Welsh

Accompanying cassette(s) are available for the above titles.
* Accompanying CDs are also available.

Colloquial
Cambodian

A Complete Language Course

David Smyth

ROUTLEDGE

London and New York

NOR

495.932

First published 1995
by Routledge
11 New Fetter Lane, London EC4P 4EE

Simultaneously published in the USA and Canada
by Routledge
29 West 35th Street, New York, NY 10001

Reprinted 1996

Routledge is an International Thomson Publishing company

Distributed exclusively in Thailand by D.K. Book House

© 1995 David Smyth

Typeset in 10/12pt Times Ten by Florencetype Ltd, Stoodleigh, Devon

Illustrations by Rebecca Moy

Printed and bound in Great Britain by Clays Ltd, St Ives plc

British Library Cataloguing in Publication Data
A catalogue record for this book is available from the British Library

Library of Congress Cataloguing in Publication Data
A catalogue record for this book is available from the Library of Congress

ISBN 0-415-10006-2 (book)
ISBN 0-415-10007-0 (cassettes)
ISBN 0-415-10008-9 (book and cassettes course)

Contents

Acknowledgements

I am deeply grateful to Mr Kien Tran for his advice and assistance during the preparation of this book. I would also like to thank Mrs Judith Jacob for her interest in the project and for her many helpful suggestions. My thanks are due to Mr John Banks, also, who has saved me from many embarrassing errors and omissions. Any errors that remain are solely my responsibility.

Introduction

General

Cambodian or *Khmer* is the national language of Cambodia, spoken by nearly eight million people within the country. Mutually intelligible dialects of Cambodian are spoken by approximately half a million people living in the Mekong Delta region of Vietnam and there are a further half million speakers in Thailand, in the northeastern provinces of Surin, Buriram and Sisaket. In Laos, the number of Cambodian speakers is much smaller, numbering little more than 10,000. Beyond South East Asia there are sizeable émigré communities of more than 50,000 in both France and USA, most of whom fled Cambodia during the 1970s.

Cambodian belongs to the Mon-Khmer language family. Most of the languages of this family are spoken in Cambodia, Vietnam, Laos and Thailand although a few are found further afield. With the exception of Cambodian, they are minority languages, often spoken in only a few villages. Cambodian is unique in enjoying the status of a national language and is one of the very few Mon-Khmer languages to have a written form and an established literary tradition.

Unlike neighbouring Vietnamese, Lao and Thai, Cambodian is not a tonal language. It does, however, share many common grammatical features with other major South East Asian languages. Word order in Cambodian follows a familiar subject + verb + object pattern. Native Cambodian words tend to consist of either one or two syllables; but a large number of foreign words have been borrowed from Sanskrit, Pali, Thai and French. For the western learner, perhaps the most notable feature of the language is the lack of verb and noun inflections; indeed, with neither complicated verb tenses nor singular and plural forms of nouns to memorise, Cambodian grammar can be absorbed relatively painlessly.

Colloquial Cambodian

This book aims to provide a practical introduction to speaking and reading Cambodian. Each lesson in the first half of the book is divided into two parts. The first part is based on dialogues and presents the grammar and vocabulary necessary to deal with everyday situations. The Cambodian script is introduced in the second part of each lesson. Each lesson from Lesson 11 onwards contains a selection of pronunciation exercises, dialogues, listening passages (which can be treated as reading passages if you do not have the cassettes that accompany this volume) and reading passages.

While it is possible to work through the dialogues ignoring the Cambodian script, the learner is strongly advised against this. A knowledge of how to read and write provides excellent reinforcement and aids the task of memorisation. It is also invaluable when trying to learn the language – or build upon existing knowledge – within the country.

How to use this course

Since Cambodian sounds quite unlike any European language, the romanisation system can offer only an approximation of how the language should be pronounced. It is therefore strongly advised that you purchase the two cassettes that accompany this course.

Each individual will probably develop their own strategies for tackling the course. You might like to start each unit by listening to the dialogue a number of times with your book closed and when you feel you can identify individual words and reproduce the sounds reasonably accurately, look at the book to find out what it was all about. Or you might feel this is a frustrating and inefficient approach and prefer to have the book open all the time. It does not really matter which approach you adopt as long as you are happy with it. As a general principle, however, it should be remembered that when learning a foreign language, 'a little and often' is more effective than lengthy but infrequent sessions.

When it comes to learning the script, copying out letters, then words, phrases and eventually whole passages will not only improve your literacy skills but will reinforce everything you have learned including pronunciation and grammar. Getting into the habit of 'doodling' in Cambodian – while watching television, on the train or in boring meetings – will help your spelling and improve your handwriting enormously. After the very first lesson start trying to recognise letters and words in the dialogues. As you become more literate, keep going back over the earlier units; reading familiar material will enable you to develop some speed and the ability to recognise words instantly without having to identify individual letters each time.

You will quickly realise that the script section in each lesson contains a considerable amount of material which needs to be absorbed before you can progress to the next lesson. To make matters worse there are a number of consonants which look very similar and a number of vowels which seem to be pronounced the same way. Perhaps the easiest way to cope with these is by making a set of handy reference cards that you can refer to while working through the lessons. (You might even photocopy the alphabet charts in Lesson 9.) In this way you can lighten the burden of pure memorisation work and you should find that over a matter of weeks you become less and less dependent on your 'crib sheet'!

Each lesson from Lesson 11 onwards contains a listening comprehension passage entitled 'Cambodian voices' in which an ordinary Cambodian talks about some aspect of their life. You might try to listen to these passages a number of times until you are sure that you can pick out the familiar words, and then check the vocabulary list for the meanings of the new words. As a further test you might try to follow the Cambodian script as you listen to the tape.

The later lessons inevitably involve introducing a considerable amount of new vocabulary which will take time to absorb. So be prepared for the fact that you will have to spend rather longer on working through each unit than you did at the beginning of the book.

Romanising Cambodian

There are a number of ways of romanising Cambodian words. The French colonial administrators developed a system during the early twentieth century and for a short-lived period during the 1940s actually decreed that it should replace the traditional Cambodian script for administrative purposes and newspapers. Many Cambodians today still romanise their names according to the French system. In the English-speaking world, learning Cambodian has tended to be restricted to an academic environment where the system of romanisation presupposes a familiarity with phonetic symbols. While the more technical system of transcription makes it possible to represent the sounds of Cambodian more accurately it can at the same time appear intimidating and complex to the learner with no background in linguistics.

The system of transcription used in this course is intended to represent Cambodian as simply as possible for the English speaker. Like all systems of transcription it is only an approximation and its purpose is simply as a crutch which the learner is advised to discard – by learning the Cambodian script – at the earliest possible moment. Since each entry is given in both romanised transcription and Cambodian script, pronunciation can be checked by asking a native speaker to read the Cambodian script entry.

The following points should be clarified:

Consonant clusters

A lot of Cambodian words begin with a consonant cluster – that is, two or more consonant sounds at the beginning of a word. Some consonant clusters, such as **sl**... and **kr**... are straightforward, as they are similar to sounds that exist in English. Others, however, such as a **l** sound after a **t** or a **ng** sound after a **ch** at first sound very strange to the western ear. These clusters are marked in the transcription with an apostrophe (e.g. **t'lai**, **ch'nguñ**, **s'rok** etc.); when pronouncing these words it is important not to insert a short **a** vowel between the two initial consonants.

Consonants

Note that **bp**, **dt**, **ng** and **ny** represent a single consonant sound.

bp   is a sharp *p* sound, somewhere between English *b* and *p* (don't actually pronounce the *b*)
      e.g. **bpee** ('two'); **bpairt** ('doctor')

dt   is a sharp *t* sound, somewhere between English *d* and *t* (don't actually pronounce the *d*)
      e.g. **dteuk** ('water'); **dtou** ('go')

j   as in 'jump'
      e.g. **joo-up** ('meet'); **jong** ('want')

g   as in 'get'
      e.g. **goy** ('customs')

ng   as in 'ring'; but note that unlike English, this sound can
      occur at the beginning of a word
      e.g. **ra-ngee-a** ('cold'); **t'ngai** ('day')

ny/ñ as in 'ca*ny*on'; but this sound can also occur at the begin-
      ning or end of a word
      e.g. **n'yum** ('eat'); **ch'nguñ** ('tasty')

Vowels

For the western learner, the Cambodian vowels are probably the
most difficult area of pronunciation. Certain vowels, so obviously
distinct to a Cambodian ear, seem totally indistinguishable, while
others seem impossible to pronounce. The important thing is not
to despair. You do not have to be able to pronounce everything
perfectly within weeks. Many language learners of modest ability
find that with perseverance their pronunciation will improve
gradually over a long period of time.
  If you can spell words in Cambodian script, it will help to clarify
the pronunciation.

-a   as in 'ago'
      e.g. **la-or** ('good')

-aa   a long *a* sound similar to English 'car', 'far' etc.
      e.g. **baan** ('can')

-ai   as in 'Thai'
      e.g. **t'lai** ('expensive') **t'ngai** ('day')

-ao   as in 'Lao'
      e.g. **gao seup** ('ninety')

-ay   as in 'pay'
      e.g. **dtay** ('question word')

-ee   as in 'see'
      e.g. **bpee** ('two')

-eu   similar to the English sound of repugnance 'ugh'! The
      Cambodian writing system distinguishes between a short
      -eu sound and a long **-eu**, but for the sake of simplicity –

and to encourage you to learn the Cambodian script – this distinction has not been made in the transcription.

e.g. **dteuk** ('water') **meun** ('10,000')

-i   as in 'fin'

e.g. **ni-yee-ay** ('speak')

-o   a short vowel similar to English 'long'

e.g. **dop** ('ten')

-oa   a long 'o' vowel similar to English 'loan', 'phone'

e.g. **goan** ('child')

-oo   a long vowel, as in 'boot'

e.g. **poom** ('village')

-ou   a short vowel

e.g. **dtou** ('go') **nou** ('live', 'be situated')

-OO   a short vowel, as in 'cook'

e.g. **yOOp** ('night')

-u   a short vowel as in 'run'

e.g. **bprum** ('five')

Where **-h** occurs at the end of the transcription (e.g. **nih** 'this', **nah** 'very') it indicates that the vowel should be pronounced with a 'breathy' voice.

Further study

This course provides you with a brief introduction to the fundamentals of spoken and written Cambodian. If you wish to develop your command of the language further you might consider working through the books below.

Modern Spoken Cambodian by Franklin E. Huffman (Yale University Press, 1970)

Cambodian System of Writing and Beginning Reader by Franklin E. Huffman (Yale University Press, 1970)

Intermediate Cambodian Reader by Franklin E. Huffman (Yale University Press, 1972)

Introduction to Cambodian by Judith M. Jacob (Oxford University Press, 1968)

If you are in Cambodia you might find all kinds of informal

language learning aids that you can consult once you can read, such as advertisements, comics, public notices, English–Cambodian phrasebooks written for Cambodian students, and so on.

Dictionaries

A Concise Cambodian–English Dictionary by Judith M. Jacob (Oxford University Press, 1974)

Cambodian–English Dictionary by Robert K. Headley, 2 vols. (Catholic University Press, 1977)

Cambodian–English Glossary by Franklin E. Huffman and Im Proum (Yale University Press, 1977)

Cambodian–English English-Cambodian Dictionary by Kem Sos, Lim Hak Kheang and Madeline E. *Ehram (sic)* [Ehrman] (Hippocrene Books, 1990)

English–Khmer Dictionary by Franklin E. Huffman and Im Proum (Yale University Press, 1978)

Practical Cambodian Dictionary (English–Cambodian, Cambodian–English) by David Smyth and Tran Kien (Charles Tuttle, 1994)

1 ni-yee-ay om-bpee kloo-un aing

Talking about yourself

In this lesson you will learn to:

- make a number of simple statements about yourself
- ask simple questions using *what*? and *where*?
- read and write some simple words and sentences

If you are a foreigner in Cambodia, your most frequent conversations with Cambodians are likely to involve telling them your name, nationality and perhaps something about your work. These are the kind of statements you will probably need to be able to make about yourself:

ni-yee-ay om-bpee kloo-un aing 🔲

k'nyom ch'moo-ah Sally.	ខ្ញុំឈ្មោះ Sally។
ch'moo-ah dtra-goal Morris.	ឈ្មោះត្រកូល Morris។
jee-a ong-klayh.	ជាអង់គ្លេស។
moak bpee lon-dorn.	មកពី London។
jee-a bpairt.	ជាពេទ្យ។
t'wer gaa nou p'nOOm bpeuñ.	ធ្វើការនៅភ្នំពេញ។

My (first) name is Sally.
My family name is Morris.
I am English.
I come from London.
I am a doctor.
I work in Phnom Penh.

Vocabulary

k'nyom	I	ខ្ញុំ
ch'moo-ah	to be named; name	ឈ្មោះ
ch'moo-ah dtra-goal	family name	ឈ្មោះត្រកូល
jee-a	is	ជា
ong-klayh	English	អង់គ្លេស
moak	come	មក
bpee	from	ពី
p'nOOm bpeuñ	Phnom Penh	ភ្នំពេញ
t'wer	to do, make	ធ្វើ
t'wer gaa	to work	ធ្វើការ
nou	to be situated at; to live at; at/in	នៅ
bpairt	doctor	ពេទ្យ

Language points

Pronouns

Cambodian has a much greater number of pronouns (e.g. you, he, she, we etc.) than English. The appropriate word depends upon the sex and relative status of the speakers. Cambodians frequently avoid using the word for 'you' and instead address a person directly by their personal name or even as 'older brother/sister' or 'younger brother/sister'. The foreigner can get by quite adequately with the limited set of pronouns set out below:

k'nyom	I, me	ខ្ញុំ
loak	you (sing./ plur.) (to address males)	លោក
loak s'ray	you (sing./ plur.) (to address older females)	លោកស្រី
nee-ung s'ray	you (sing./ plur.) (to address younger females)	នាងស្រី
goa-ut	he, she, they	គាត់
gay	he, she, they	គេ
yerng	we, us	យើង

However, pronouns are frequently omitted when it is obvious who is being referred to. Thus, when talking about yourself, you do not have to begin each sentence with **k'nyom**.

What . . .? questions ▭▭

The Cambodian word for 'what?' is **ay?**, sometimes pronounced **a-way?**. By contrast with English, it comes at the end of the sentence:

loak ch'moo-ah *ay?* លោកឈ្មោះ អ្វី?
What's your name?

loak ch'moo-ah dtra-goal *ay?* លោកឈ្មោះ ត្រកូល អ្វី?
What's your surname?

loak jee-a joo-un jee-ut *ay?* លោកជាជនជាតិ អ្វី?
What's your nationality?

loak t'wer gaa *ay*? លោកធ្វើការ អ្វី?
What do you do? (*What's* your job?)

Where . . .? questions 🔲🔲

The word for 'where?' in Cambodian is **ai-naa?**, alternatively pronounced **ee-naa?**; this question word also appears at the end of the sentence:

goa-ut nou *ee-naa*? គាត់នៅឯណា?
Where does he live? / *Where* is he?

goa-ut t'wer gaa nou *ee-naa*? គាត់ធ្វើការ នៅឯណា?
Where does he work?

But notice that **ai/ee** (which means 'at') is dropped when asking where someone comes from:

goa-ut moak bpee *naa*? គាត់មកពីណា?
Where does he come *from*?

Names

In Cambodian, the family name comes before the given name. School pupils are normally addressed by teacher and classmates by the equivalent of *Smith John* or *Smith Jane*. Given names may be used between close friends.

In adulthood a man is referred to with the respectful title **loak** followed by either the family name and given name (**loak Smith John**) or just the given name (**loak John**).

Unmarried woman are referred to or addressed in the same way except that the title **nee-ung** is used rather than **loak** (i.e. **nee-ung Smith Jane** or **nee-ung Jane**); for married women, the appropriate term of address is **nay-uk s'ray** or **loak s'ray**, again followed by the family name and then the personal name (i.e. **nay-uk s'ray Smith Mary** or **loak s'ray Smith Mary**). When dealing with westerners, some Cambodians may reverse the order of family and personal names to fit in with the western convention!

Seeking confirmation

The words **. . . mairn dtay?** – which can be roughly translated as 'isn't that so?' – can be tagged on to the end of a statement to confirm that we have understood something or made the correct assumption. It is particularly useful for learners as it provides a welcome alternative strategy to 'Pardon?' There are several ways of saying 'yes' in Cambodian, but if you've got it right, you'll probably hear either **baat** (if it's a male) or **jaa** (if it's a female). In Lesson 3 you will learn another way of responding to **mairn dtay?** questions.

A: **loak moak bpee naa?** លោកមកពីណា?
   Where do you come from?

B: **k'nyom moak bpee dtaa gai-o.** ខ្ញុំមកពីតាកែវ ។
   I come from Takéo.

A: **dtaa gai-o** *mairn dtay*? តាកែវមែនទេ?
   Takéo, *right*?

B: **baat.** ប្រាទ ។
   Yes.

Exercise 1

Suppose a Cambodian asks you these questions; how would you respond?

1 loak ch'moo-ah ay? លោកឈ្មោះ អ្វី?

2 loak jee-a joo-un jee-ut ay? លោកជាជនជាតិអ្វី ?

3 loak moak bpee naa? លោកមកពីណា?

4 loak t'wer gaa ay? (*If you don't know the word, use English*) លោកធ្វើការ អ្វី?

5 loak t'wer gaa nou ee-naa? លោកធ្វើការ នៅឯណា?

Exercise 2

Write questions to fit the following answers:

A: ...
B: k'nyom ch'moo-ah Sok. ខ្ញុំឈ្មោះ សុខ។
A: ...
B: moak bpee but-dtom-borng. មកពីប្រាត់តំបង។
A: ...
B: jee-a nay-uk jOOm-noo-uñ (businessman). ជាអ្នកជំនួញ។

A: ...

B: twer gaa nou p'nOOm bpeuñ. ធ្វើការ នៅភ្នំពេញ ។

Exercise 3

How would you say the following in Cambodian:

1 What's your name?
2 My name is Som Sok.
3 A: Your family name is Som, right? B: Yes.
4 Where do you come from?
5 I come from Takéo.
6 Where do you work?
7 I work in Phnom Penh.
8 I'm a doctor.

Mom 🔲

Read the following short 'biography' of a girl called Mom. Where does she come from and what is she doing now?

Vocabulary

k'mai	Khmer	ខ្មែរ
but-dtom-borng	Battambang	ប្រាត់តំបង
ni(h)-seut	student	និស្សិត
ree-un	to study	រៀន
pee-a-saa	language	ភាសា

k'nyom ch'moo-ah Mom.	ខ្ញុំឈ្មោះ ម៉ុំ។
ch'moo-ah dtra-goal mee-ah.	ឈ្មោះ ត្រកូល មាស ។
jee-a k'mai.	ជាខ្មែរ ។
k'nyom moak bpee but-dtom-borng.	ខ្ញុំមកពីបាត់តំបង ។
jee-a nih-seut.	ជានិស្សិត ។
ree-un pee-a-saa ong-klayh.	រៀនភាសាអង់គ្លេស ។
ree-un nou p'nOOm bpeuñ.	រៀននៅភ្នំពេញ ។

Script

The Cambodian system of writing

Cambodian is written across the page from left to right. The Cambodian alphabet, although unique to Cambodia, bears some close similarities to the Thai and Lao alphabets. All have developed from an alphabet that originated in south India.

In Cambodia there are two distinct styles of script – **uk-sor ch'ree-ung** or 'slanted script' and **uk-sor mool** or 'rounded script'. The former is the most common and that used in this book. Newspapers, books and all typewritten material use this form of script. The more ornate rounded script is used for headings in public notices, names of buildings, titles of books and so on.

There are no spaces between words in Cambodian; when spaces do occur in Cambodian writing, they serve as punctuation marks, rather like commas. Certain vowel symbols appear above the consonant, rather than after it, while others are written beneath, in front of, or even surrounding the consonant on three sides. A further unusual feature for the westerner is that when two consonants occur at the beginning of a word – for example in the word **srok** – the second consonant is written using a special subscript form *beneath* the first consonant.

Consonants

The consonants in this lesson and those that follow are presented not in the normal Cambodian alphabetical order (which appears in

Lesson 9) but in an order which is designed to help you read Cambodian as quickly as possible.

Cambodian consonants are classified as belonging to either the **first series** (sometimes called **first register**) or **second series** (or **second register**). Since the *series* or *register* of the initial consonant in a word will determine how that word is pronounced, it is essential to remember which series each consonant belongs to. All of the consonants in this lesson are **second series** consonants.

ន	ម	ង	ញ
n	m	ng	ñ/ny

រ	យ	ល	វ
r	y	l	w*

* Some Cambodians pronounce this consonant similarly to English *v*.

Vowels

Nearly every vowel symbol or configuration has *two* possible pronunciations in Cambodian – a '*first series* pronunciation' used when the preceding consonant belongs to the first series, and a '*second series* pronunciation' used when the preceding consonant belongs to the second series. There are three vowel symbols that are pronounced the same regardless of the series of the initial consonant.

Since the consonants in this unit are all *second series* consonants, the vowel symbols introduced below are, for the moment, given only with their *second series* values.

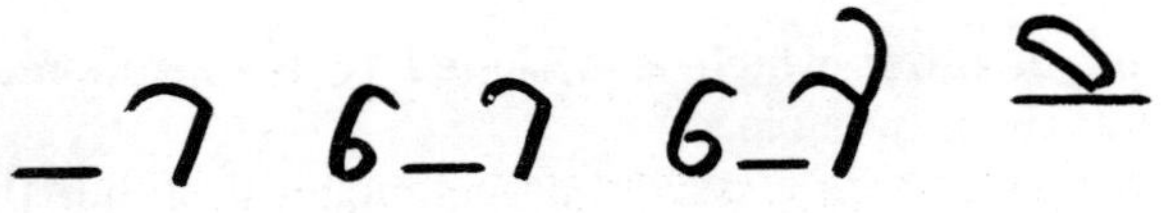

-ា	េ-ា	េ-ៅ	ិ
-ee-a	-oa	-ou	-i/eu*

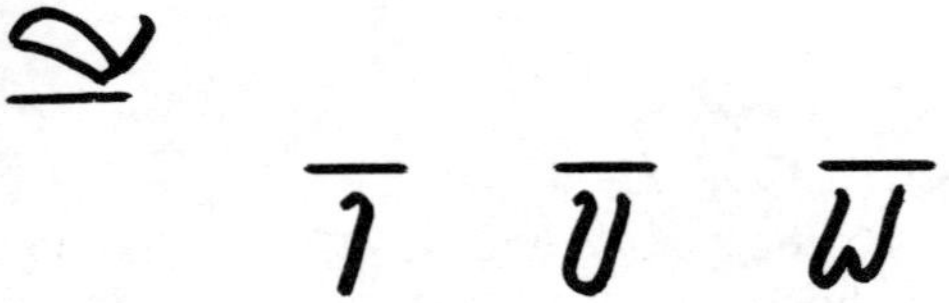

ី	ុ	ូ	ួ
-ee	-OO	-oo	-oo-a

(Note that the hyphen (-) is not a part of the vowel symbol, but merely indicates the position of the consonant in relation to that vowel symbol.)

* This vowel symbol is a little erratic! When ិ is followed by a final consonant it is usually pronounced **-eu**, e.g. មិន **meun**.

Exercise 4

See how many letters you can now recognise in this sample of Cambodian script. The symbol ។, as you might have guessed, represents a full stop.

នៅថ្ងៃទី ១៧ មេសា ១៩៧៥ ប្រហែលរសៀលម៉ោង ២ ពួក
ទាហានខ្មែរក្រហមមកដល់ផ្ទះខ្ញុំ ប្រាប់ខ្ញុំថា អាមេរិកាំងនឹង
មកទម្លាក់គ្រាប់បែកភ្លាម ៗ នេះហើយចូរចេញពីផ្ទះភ្លាម ។
ខ្ញុំសួរថា លោកត្រូវការឲ្យខ្ញុំទៅកន្លែងណា ? ប៉ុន្មានថ្ងៃ
ទៀតឲ្យខ្ញុំមកផ្ទះវិញ ? ខ្មែរក្រហមម្នាក់ឆ្លើយថា ចេញតាម
ទិសខាងជើងតែ ២ ឬ ៣ ថ្ងៃប៉ុណ្ណោះ គេនឹងអនុញ្ញាតឲ្យ

មកផ្ទះវិញហើយ ។ ខ្ញុំជឿលើពាក្យដែលពួកនេះនិយាយទាំង
អស់ ក៏ម្ល៉ោះព្រោះប្រពន្ធខ្ញុំឲ្យរៀបចាំសម្លៀកបំពាក់ នឹងយក
ស្បៀងអាហារ ខ្លះព្រមទាំងចានឆ្នាំងបន្តិចបន្តួចតែប៉ុណ្ណោះ
តាមខ្លួន ។

Exercise 5

This exercise combines the consonants and vowels into some common words. At this stage, however, we do not need to worry about
meanings. The aim of the exercise is simply to get used to producing
the correct sounds! If you have the cassette that accompanies this
course, listen to the exercise and follow it in the book.

នៅ	នាង	មាន	លាន	រោង
រាល	លា	រ៉ា	មីង	មិន
មុន	លុយ	យួរ *	ម្លុយ	យុន
យាយ	លារ់	នារ៉ី	និម្លុយ	និយាយ

*យួរ A final 'r' is not pronounced in standard Cambodian. Read
the word as if it were យួ. The spelling probably reflects an archaic
pronunciation which survives in Cambodian dialects spoken in parts
of western Cambodia and north-east Thailand.

Exercise 6

And already we can start to build up some meaningful sentences!
(Although a list of words used is given after the sentences, don't
worry about trying to understand the sentences or memorise the
new words at this stage; the main object of this exercise is to get
used to the idea of spotting where one word ends and the next
begins.)

1 លុយ មានលុយ មិនមានលុយ នាងមិនមានលុយ
2 យួរ នៅយួរ មិននៅយួរ មីងមិននៅយួរ

3 យួន   នាយយួន   លានាយយួន   នាងលានាយយួន

Vocabulary

លុយ	money	មីង	aunt
មាន	have	យួន	Vietnamese
មិន	not	នាយ	boss
នាង	'Miss'	លា	leave
យូរ	a long time	មួយ	one
នៅ	live; be situated (at)		

2 ni-yee-ay om-bpee kroo-a-saa (1)

Talking about your family (1)

> **In this lesson you will learn about:**
> - the question word . . . **dtay?**
> - numbers 1–10
> - some *first series* consonants

Once Cambodians know that you speak a little of their language they will usually want to find out all about you and your family. While it would be unusual to be asking a new English acquaintance how many brothers and sisters he or she had, it is an extremely common question for foreigners to be faced with in Cambodia, as in most parts of South East Asia.

ni-yee-ay om-bpee kroo-a-saa (1) 🔲

> A: Cambodian; B: visitor

A:	mee-un borng bpa-oan dtay?	មានបងប្អូនទេ?
B:	jaa, mee-un bprum nay-uk.	ចាំ មានប្រាំនាក់។
	mee-un borng bproh m'nay-uk	មានបងប្រុសម្នាក់
	borng s'ray bpee	បងស្រីពីរ
	bpa-oan bproh moo-ay hai-ee neung	ប្អូនប្រុសសម្បួយហើយនឹង
	bpa-oan s'ray moo-ay.	ប្អូនស្រីមួយ ។
A:	mee-un roop tort dtay?	មានរូបថតទេ?
B:	jaa, mee-un.	ចាំ មាន ។

nih oa-bpOOk m'dai neung   នេះខ្ពុកម្ដាយនឹ

borng bpa-oan k'nyom.   បងប្អូនខ្ញុំ ។

A: *Do you have any brothers and sisters?*
B: *Yes, I have five.*
   I have one older brother, two older sisters,
   one younger brother and one younger sister.
A: *Do you have any photos?*
B: *Yes, I do.*
   These are my parents and
   brothers and sisters.

Vocabulary

mee-un	to have; there is/are	មាន
borng bpa-oan	brothers and sisters	បងប្អូន
. . . dtay?	*question word*	. . . ទេ?
jaa	yes (female speaker)	ចា៎
bprum	five	ប្រាំ
nay-uk	*classifier*	នាក់
borng bproh	older brother	បងប្រុស
moo-ay	one	មួយ
borng s'ray	older sister	បងស្រី
bpee	two	ពីរ
bpa-oan bproh	younger brother	ប្អូនប្រុស
hai-ee neung; neung	and	ហើយនឹង ; នឹង
bpa-oan s'ray	younger sister	ប្អូនស្រី
roop tort	photograph	រូបថត
nih	this, this is	នេះ
oa-bpOOk m'dai	parents	ខ្ពុកម្ដាយ
oa-bpOOk	father	ខ្ពុក
m'dai	mother	ម្ដាយ

Language points

Question word . . . dtay?

The word . . . **dtay?** can be tagged on to the end of a statement or sentence to turn it into a question. Unlike . . . **mairn dtay?** (see Lesson 1), it is a neutral question form with no built in assumption about what the answer will be:

tom ('big') *dtay?*	*Is it* big?	ធំ ទេ?
t'lai ('expensive') *dtay?*	*Is it* expensive?	ថ្លៃ ទេ?
ch'ngai ('far') *dtay?*	*Is it* far?	ឆ្ងាយ ទេ?

To answer 'yes' to a . . . **dtay?** question, repeat the main verb in the question; you can add the word **baat** (male speakers) or **jaa** (female speakers) for extra politeness:

tom dtay?	Is it big?	ធំ ទេ?
baat, tom	Yes.	បាទ ធំ
t'lai dtay?	Is it expensive?	ថ្លៃ ទេ?
jaa, t'lai	Yes.	ចា ថ្លៃ

To answer 'no' to a . . . **dtay?** question, you say **dtay** (which confusingly for the learner means 'no' as well as being a question word), or more politely, **baat, dtay** (male speakers) or **jaa, dtay** (female speakers). In negative responses, **baat** and **jaa** are simply polite acknowledgements of the speaker's question; in effect they mean 'I've heard your question and my answer will follow shortly'!

tom dtay?	Is it big?	ធំ ទេ?
baat, dtay	No.	បាទ ទេ។
t'lai dtay?	Is it expensive?	ថ្លៃ ទេ?
jaa, dtay	No.	ចា ទេ។

Brothers and sisters

When talking about brothers and sisters in Cambodian, you always
have to specify whether you are referring to someone who is older
or younger than you. The word **borng** is used for older siblings and
bpa-oan for younger siblings. One of these words is then combined
with the word for male (**bproh**) or female (**s'ray**), although often a
Cambodian will refer to a member of their family simply as **borng**
and the listener may not know whether the speaker is referring to a
male or a female. The term for brothers and sisters, **borng bpa-oan**,
literally means 'older ones younger ones' without specifying any
gender.

Numbers

Here are the Cambodian numbers from 1 to 10. Later in the lesson
you will learn how to write the numerals in Cambodian script.
Notice that the words for *six, seven, eight* etc. are literally 'five-one',
'five-two' 'five-three' etc. Of the two words for *seven* **bprum-bpeul** is
the more colloquial. The Cambodian written form, however,
reflects only the formal pronunciation of the word.

one	**moo-ay**	មួយ
two	**bpee**	ពីរ
three	**bay**	បី
four	**boo-un**	បួន
five	**bprum**	ប្រាំ
six	**bprum moo-ay**	ប្រាំមួយ
seven	**bprum bpee**	ប្រាំពីរ
	or **bprum-bpeul**	
eight	**bprum bay**	ប្រាំបី
nine	**bprum boo-un**	ប្រាំបួន
ten	**dop**	ដប់

Using nouns with numbers

There is no separate plural form for nouns in Cambodian. The
number word occurs after the noun unless it is a unit of time (e.g.
day, week, year) or a unit of measure (e.g. metre, kilogram, etc.).
However, when the noun is a human being the word **nay-uk**
('person') is added:

borng s'ray bpee nay-uk   two older sisters   បងស្រីពីរនាក់

bpairt dop nay-uk   ten doctors   ពេទ្យដប់នាក់

Usually, when the word **moo-ay** ('one') is used with a classifier it is
contracted to **m'** (+ classifier):

borng bproh m'nay-uk   one older brother   បងប្រុសម្នាក់

As you will see from the dialogue, however, Cambodians do not use
nay-uk slavishly and it can be dropped quite naturally.

The word **nay-uk** is termed a *classifier* or *'count word'*. Classifiers
are common in many South East Asian languages. While a number
of other classifiers are used in formal Cambodian, they are much
less commonly used in the spoken language.

Possessive

The word for 'of' is **ra-boh**, and possession can be expressed using
the pattern noun + **ra-boh** + possessor. In normal speech, however,
ra-boh is frequently omitted:

borng s'ray *ra-boh* k'nyom   បងស្រីរបស់ខ្ញុំ

or **borng s'ray k'nyom**   បងស្រីខ្ញុំ
My older sister ('older sister-of-I')

oa-bpOOk m'dai *ra-boh* yerng   ខ្ញុំពុកម្ដាយរបស់យើង

or **oa-bpOOk m'dai yerng**   ខ្ញុំពុកម្ដាយយើង
Our parents ('parents-of-we')

There are no special possessive pronouns in Cambodian to corre-
spond to English 'mine', 'yours', 'his' etc.

Exercise 1 📼

This is a picture of Sally with her brothers and sisters.

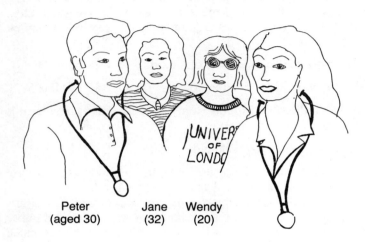

Peter   Jane   Wendy
(aged 30)   (32)   (20)

How should she answer if a Cambodian friend asks her these questions:

1 mee-un borng-bpa-oan dtay?   មានបងប្អូនទេ?

2 mee-un borng s'ray dtay?   មានបងស្រីទេ?

3 borng s'ray ch'moo-ah ay?   បងស្រីឈ្មោះ អ្វី?

4 borng bproh t'wer gaa ay?   បងប្រុសធ្វើការ អ្វី?

5 bpa-oan s'ray ree-un nou ee-naa?   ប្អូនស្រីរៀននៅឯណា?

Exercise 2

Now draw a picture of your family and say as much as you can about each person! You might want to begin like this . . .

nih m'dai k'nyom.
ch'moo-ah Mary.
moak bpee Liverpool.
t'wer gaa nou London . . .

Exercise 3

How would you say the following in Cambodian:

1 Do you have any brothers and sisters?
2 Yes, I have three brothers and sisters.
3 I have an older sister and two younger brothers.
4 Do you have a photograph?
5 Yes. This is my older sister.
6 What is your older sister's name?
7 Where does your father work?
8 Where does your mother come from?

kroo-a-saa k'nyom
My family ▣

Here is another short 'biography' in which a survivor of the
Cambodian holocaust describes his family.

Vocabulary

gart	to be born	កើត
s'rok	country	ស្រុក
jeun	China, Chinese	ចិន
s'rok jeun	China	ស្រុកចិន
dtai	but; only	តែ
yoo	a long time	យូរ
kait	province	ខេត្ត
saam seup	thirty	សាមសិប
ch'num	year	ឆ្នាំ
geu	is; that is; namely	គឺ
ay-lou nih	now	ឥឡូវនេះ
s'lup	to die	ស្លាប់
bpayl	period of time	ពេល
bpol bpot	Pol Pot	ប៉ុល ពត

oa-bpOOk gart nou s'rok jeun dtai nou

ខ្ញុំពូកកើតនៅស្រុកចិន តែនៅ

s'rok k'mai yoo. m'dai jee-a k'mai.

ស្រុកខ្មែរយូរ ។ ម្ដាយជាខ្មែរ ។

moak bpee kait gom-bpoo-ung jaam.

មកពីខេត្តកំពង់ចាម ។

oa-bpOOk m'dai nou p'nOOm bpeuñ

ខ្ញុំពូកម្ដាយនៅភ្នំពេញ

saam seup ch'num. k'nyom mee-un

សាមសិបឆ្នាំ ។ ខ្ញុំមាន

borng-bpa-oan bprum-moo-ay nay-uk.

បងប្អូនប្រាំមួយនាក់ ។

geu mee-un borng s'ray bpee, borng

គឺមានបងស្រីពីរ បង

bproh bpee, bpa-oan bproh m'nay-uk

ប្រុសពីរ ប្អូនប្រុសម្នាក់

hai-ee neung bpa-oan s'ray m'nay-uk.

ហើយនឹងប្អូនស្រីម្នាក់ ។

ay-lou nih oa-bpOOk m'dai neung

ឥឡូវនេះ ខ្ញុំពូកម្ដាយនឹង

borng-bpa-oan bprum nay-uk s'lup

បងប្អូនប្រាំនាក់ស្លាប់

hai-ee. s'lup bpayl bpol bpot.

ហើយ ។ ស្លាប់ពេលប៉ុល ពត ។

Script

Consonants

All of the consonants in this unit are *first series* (or *second register*) consonants.

ក	ខ	ច	ឆ	ដ
ក	ខ	ច	ឆ	ដ
g	k	j	ch	d

ត	ថ	ប	ផ
ត	ថ	ប *	ផ
dt	t	b	p

* Note that when ប is followed by the vowel -ា a special symbol បា is used to represent the sound **baa**; this is to avoid confusion with the consonant ហ (*h*) – which we shall meet shortly.

Vowels

When the vowel symbols that you learned in the last lesson are combined with *first series* consonants they are pronounced as follows: (*second series* pronunciations are given below for reference; note that the vowel symbol -ួ retains the same pronunciation for both *first* and *second series* consonants).

-ា	ោ-	ៅ-	-ិ	-ី	-ុ	-ូ	-ួ
-aa	-ao	-ao	-e*	-ay	-o	-oa	-oo-a
(-ee-a	-oa	-ou	-i/eu	-ee	-OO	-oo	-oo-a)

* This vowel symbol is again somewhat unpredictable! When ◌̎ occurs with a *first series* consonant and is followed by a final consonant it is usually pronounced -eu, e.g. បិន **jeun.**

Numbers

In the first part you learned how to count from 1 to 10 in Cambodian. This is how the numbers are written. (Numbers 1–10 are written the same way in neighbouring Thailand and Laos.)

១	២	៣	៤	៥
1	2	3	4	5

៦	៧	៨	៩	១០
6	7	8	9	10

Exercise 4

Here is the same sample of script that you met in Lesson 1. See how many letters you can pick out now.

នៅថ្ងៃទី ១៧ មេសា ១៩៧៥ ប្រហែលរសៀលម៉ោង ២ ពួក ទាហានខ្មែរក្រហមមកដល់ផ្ទះខ្ញុំ ប្រាប់ខ្ញុំថា អាមេរិកាំងនឹង មកទម្លាក់គ្រាប់បែកភ្លាម ៗ នេះហើយចូរចេញពីផ្ទះភ្លាម ៤ ខ្ញុំសួរថា លោកត្រូវការឲ្យខ្ញុំទៅកន្លែងណា ? ប៉ុន្មានថ្ងៃ ទៀតឲ្យខ្ញុំមកផ្ទះវិញ ? ខ្មែរក្រហមម្នាក់ឆ្លើយថា ចេញតាម

ទិសខាងជើងតែ ២ ឬ ៣ ថ្ងៃប៉ុណ្ណោះ គេនឹងអនុញ្ញាតឲ្យ
មកផ្ទះវិញហើយ ។ ខ្ញុំជឿលើពាក្យដែលពួកនេះនិយាយទាំង
អស់ ក៏ម្ដិម្មាប្រាប់ប្រពន្ធខ្ញុំឲ្យរៀបចាំសម្លៀកបំពាក់ និងយក
ស្បៀងអាហារ ខ្លះ ព្រមទាំងចានឆ្នាំងបន្ដិចបន្ដួចតែប៉ុណ្ណោះ
តាមខ្លួន ។

Exercise 5

All of these words begin with *first series* consonants.

កា	ខោ	ចៅ	គា	ជី
ចាយ	ជ្រាយ	បី	ហ្ន	កូន
ខាង	ថា	ខាន	ជ្រាន	គាម
ដូន	កាល	ចាម	កោង	ជ្រាវ៍ *

*This is an irregular pronunciation: you might expect **baa-ree**; in fact it is **baa-ray**.

Exercise 6

What are these telephone numbers?

1 ២ ៥៣៧១

2 ២ ៦០៤៩

3 ២ ០៨២៣

4 ២ ៧៩៨១

5 ២ ៨៦៥៧

Exercise 7

Here are some more short sentences. Again, although vocabulary is given below, don't worry about memorising it or not understanding the grammar; the object of the exercise is purely to familiarise you with the idea of words being run together. If it helps, you can draw a faint dotted line to mark the word boundaries; within a short time, however, you will find you can largely dispense with this strategy.

1 មុខ ខាងមុខ នៅខាងមុខ ចាននៅខាងមុខ
2 ប៉ារី មានប៉ារី មិនមានប៉ារី តាមិនមានប៉ារី
3 ដូន តាមដូន កូនតាមដូន កូនម៉ីងតាមដូន
4 ចាយ ប្រានចាយ មិនប្រានចាយ តាមិនប្រានចាយ
5 ប្រាន មិនប្រាន និយាយមិនប្រាន និយាយចិនមិនប្រាន

Vocabulary

មុខ	face, front	កូន	child
ខាង	side	ម៉ីង	aunt
នៅ	to be at	ចាយ	to pay
ចាន	plate	ប្រាន	can; past time marker
ប៉ារី	cigarette	ប្រានចាយ	have paid
មាន	to have	តា	grandfather, old man
មិន	not	មិនប្រាន	can't
ដូន	old lady	និយាយ	to speak
តាម	to follow	ចិន	Chinese

3 ni-yee-ay om-bpee kroo-a-saa (2)

Talking about your family (2)

In this lesson you will learn about:

- *who?* and *how many?* questions
- negatives
- past tense marker **hai-ee**
- numbers 11–20
- words with no written vowel symbol

Family snapshots are excellent ice-breakers; if they are your own photographs, you can rehearse what you are going to say about the characters in each picture beforehand and practise the same conversation on every native speaker willing to listen to you; and if they are someone else's pictures you can use a few stock questions. Here's Sally asking a Cambodian friend about some of her photos.

ni-yee-ay om-bpee kroo-a-saa (2) 📼

A: Sally; B: Cambodian friend

A:	nih borng bproh mairn dtay?	នេះបងប្រុសមែនទេ?
B:	meun mairn dtay.	មិនមែនទេ។
	nOOh b'day borng s'ray.	នោះប្ដីបងស្រី។
A:	hai-ee neung nih nay-uk naa?	ហើយនឹងនេះ អ្នកណា?
B:	nih borng neung goan s'ray moo-ay.	
		នេះបងនឹងកូនស្រីម្នួយ។

A: sa-aat nah.　　　　　　　　　　ស្អាតណាស់ ។

mee-un goan bpon-maan nay-uk?　មានកូនប៉ុន្នាននាក់?

B: jaa mee-un goan bpay nay-uk.　ចាំ មានកូនបីនាក់ ។

goan bproh m'nay-uk　　　　　　កូនប្រុសម្នាក់

goan s'ray bpee.　　　　　　　　កូនស្រីពីរ ។

A: aa-yOO bpon-maan?　　　　　　អាយុប៉ុន្នាន?

B: goan bproh aa-yOO dop　　　　កូនប្រុសអាយុ១០

ch'num hai-ee　　　　　　　　　ឆ្នាំហើយ

goan s'ray dtee moo-ay bprum ch'num　កូនស្រីទិម្ពុយ ៥ ឆ្នាំ

goan s'ray dtee bpee boo-un ch'num.　កូនស្រីទិពីរ ៤ ឆ្នាំ ។

A: bpa-oan s'ray gaa hai-ee　　　ប្អូនស្រីការ ហើយ

mairn dtay?　　　　　　　　　　មែនទេ ?

B: mairn hai-ee.　　　　　　　　មែនហើយ ។

gaa bprum ch'num hai-ee　　　ការ ប្រាំឆ្នាំ ហើយ

bpon-dtai k'mee-un goan dtay.　ប៉ុន្តែគ្មានកូនទេ ។

A: *This is your older brother, isn't it?*
B: *No.*
　That's my older sister's husband.
A: *And who's this?*
B: *This is my older (brother) and one of his
　daughters.*
A: *She's lovely.*

How many children do they have?
B: *They've got three children.*
   One son (and) two daughters.
A: *How old are they?*
B: *The son is ten years old.*
   The first daughter is five,
   the second daughter four.
A: *Your younger sister is married, isn't she?*
B: *That's right.*
   She's been married five years.
   But she doesn't have any children.

Vocabulary

nOOh	that, that is	នោះ
nah	very	ណាស់
nay-uk naa?	who?	អ្នកណា?
b'day	husband	ប្ដី
goan	child	កូន
goan s'ray	daughter	កូនស្រី
sa-aat	beautiful; clean	ស្អាត
bpon-maan?	how many?	ប៉ុន្មាន?
goan bproh	son	កូនប្រុស
m'nay-uk	*one person*	ម្នាក់
aa-yOO	age; to be . . . years old	អាយុ
dtee moo-ay	first	ទីមួយ
dtee bpee	second	ទីពីរ
gaa	to be married	ការ
hai-ee	already	ហើយ
bpon-dtai	but	ប៉ុន្តែ
k'mee-un	not have, there aren't	គ្មាន
meun . . . dtay	not	មិន . . . ទេ

Language points

. . . mairn dtay? *questions* 🔲

This tag question appeared in Lesson 1 as a useful way of seeking confirmation; in that lesson, the questioner's assumptions were confirmed by the answer **baat** or **jaa**. Another way of saying 'yes' to a **. . . mairn dtay?** question is **mairn** or **mairn hai-ee**.

In this lesson, the first question in the conversation makes a wrong assumption, prompting the negative response, **meun mairn dtay** ('no'/'that is not so').

Negatives

The negative is formed by putting **meun** in front of the main verb (and remember that words like 'big', 'expensive', 'far' etc. are verbs in Cambodian) and, optionally, **dtay** after it.

meun* tom *dtay	*not* big	មិនធំទេ
meun* t'lai *dtay	*not* expensive	មិនថ្លៃទេ

The negative of **mee-un** ('to have'), however, is **k'mee-un**:

k'nyom *k'mee-un dtay*	I *don't* have (any).	ខ្ញុំក្មានទេ។

Who? *questions*

The position of **nay-uk naa** ('who?') varies according to the question:

nay-uk naa **bprup** ('to tell') **goa-ut?** អ្នកណាប្រាប់គាត់?
Who told him?

yerng dtou joo-up ('to meet') **nay-uk naa?** យើងទៅជួបអ្នកណា?
Who are we going to meet?

How many? *questions* 🔲

The question word **bpon-maan** ('how much?', 'how many?') occurs after the main verb and can be followed by a classifier, such as **nay-uk** when asking about people, or a unit of measurement.

mee-un goan *bpon-maan* nay-uk? មានកូនប៉ុន្មាននាក់?
How many children do you have?

aa-yOO *bpon-maan* (ch'num)?		អាយុប៉ុន្មាន (ឆ្នាំ)?
How old are they?		

Ordinal numbers

Ordinal numbers are formed by adding the word **dtee** in front of the cardinal number:

dtee moo-ay	first	ទីមួយ
dtee bpee	second ...	ទីពីរ
dtee dop	tenth *etc.*	ទីដប់

Past time marker hai-ee

The word **hai-ee** basically means 'already'. It appears after the main verb and indicates the action of the verb has been completed:

goa-ut dtou hai-ee	គាត់ទៅហើយ។
He's gone.	
yerng n'yum bai ('to eat') **hai-ee**	យើងញ៉ាំបាយហើយ ។
We've eaten.	
k'nyom deung ('to know') **hai-ee**	ខ្ញុំដឹងហើយ។
I know.	

Numbers 11–20

eleven	**dop moo-ay** (*formal*)	ដប់មួយ	១១
	or **moo-ay don-dop** (*colloquial*)	មួយដណ្ដប់	
twelve	**dop bpee**	ដប់ពីរ	១២
	or **bpee don-dop**	ពីរដណ្ដប់	
Thirteen	**dop bay**	ដប់បី	១៣
	or **bay don-dop**	បីដណ្ដប់	
Fourteen	**dop boo-un**	ដប់បួន	១៤
	or **boo-un don-dop**	បួនដណ្ដប់	
Fifteen	**dop bprum**	ដប់ប្រាំ	១៥

	or **bprum don-dop**	ប្រាំដណ្ដប់	
Sixteen	**dop bprum moo-ay**	ដប់ប្រាំមួយ	១៦
	or **bprum-moo-ay don-dop**	ប្រាំមួយដណ្ដប់	
Seventeen	**dop bprum bpee**	ដប់ប្រាំពីរ	១៧
	or **dop bprum-bpeul**		
	or **bprum-bpeul don-dop**	ប្រាំពីរដណ្ដប់	
Eighteen	**dop bprum bay**	ដប់ប្រាំបី	១៨
	or **bprum-bay don-dop**	ប្រាំបីដណ្ដប់	
Nineteen	**dop bprum boo-un**	ដប់ប្រាំបួន	១៩
	or **bprum boo-un don-dop**	ប្រាំបួនដណ្ដប់	
Twenty	**m'pay**	ម្ភៃ	២០

Exercise 1

This is a picture of Sok with his elder brother, aged 20, his elder sister (17) and his younger sister (7).

1 **Sok mee-un borng bpa-oan**
   bpon-maan nay-uk?

សុខមានបងប្អូន
ប៉ុន្មាននាក់?

2 **borng bproh aa-yOO bpon-maan?**

បងប្រុសអាយុប៉ុន្មាន?

3 **bpa-oan s'ray aa-yOO**
   bpon-maan?

ប្អូនស្រីអាយុ
ប៉ុន្មាន?

4 oa-bpOOk m'dai mee-un goan ឪពុកម្ដាយមានកូន
bpon-maan nay-uk ប៉ុន្មាននាក់?

5 mee-un goan s'ray m'nay-uk មានកូនស្រីម្នាក់
mairn dtay? មែនទេ?

Exercise 2

If a Cambodian asked you these questions, how would you respond?

1 ch'moo-a ay? ឈ្មោះអ្វី?

2 moak bpee naa? មកពីណា?

3 aa-yOO bpon-maan? អាយុប៉ុន្មាន?

4 mee-un borng bpa-oan dtay? មានបងប្អូនទេ?

5 mee-un borng bpa-oan bpon-maan nay-uk?

មានបងប្អូនប៉ុន្មាននាក់?

6 gaa hai-ee mairn dtay? ការហើយមែនទេ?

7 gaa bpon-maan ch'num hai-ee? ការប៉ុន្មានឆ្នាំហើយ?

Exercise 3

How would you say the following in Cambodian:

1 That's your sister's husband, isn't it?
2 No, that's my brother.
3 How many brothers and sisters do you have?
4 How many children do you have?
5 I have one daughter and two sons.
6 How old is your daughter? What's her name?

goan k'nyom
My children

In this passage a Cambodian tells you a little about his family. What does he say about his wife? And how old are his children?

Vocabulary

bpra-bpoo-un	wife	ប្រពន្ធ
tai	Thai	ថៃ
baang-gork	Bangkok	ប៉ាងកក
bpra-hail	about	ប្រហែល
dtay-ung	all	ទាំង
dtay-ung bpee	both	ទាំងពីរ

k'nyom gaa dop bprum ch'num
hai-ee. bpra-bpoo-un k'nyom
jee-a tai moak bpee baang-gork.
yerng nou s'rok nih bpra-hail
dop ch'num hai-ee. mee-un goan
bay nay-uk. goan s'ray aa-yOO
dop boo-un ch'num hai-ee. gart
nou s'rok tai. goan bproh
dtay-ung bpee gart nou s'rok
nih. goan bproh dtee moo-ay
aa-yOO dop moo-ay hai-ee neung
goan bproh dtee bpee aa-yOO
dop ch'num.

ខ្ញុំការដប់ប្រាំឆ្នាំ
ហើយ ។ ប្រពន្ធខ្ញុំ
ជាថៃ មកពីប៉ាងកក ។
យើងនៅស្រុកនេះប្រហែល
ដប់ឆ្នាំហើយ ។ មានកូន
បីនាក់ ។ កូនស្រីអាយុ
ដប់បួនឆ្នាំហើយ ។ កើត
នៅស្រុកថៃ ។ កូនប្រុស
ទាំងពីរ កើតនៅស្រុក
នេះ ។ កូនប្រុសទីមួយ
អាយុដប់មួយ ហើយនឹង
កូនប្រុសទីពីរ អាយុ
ដប់ឆ្នាំ ។

Script

Consonants

All of the consonants in this unit are *second series* or *second register* consonants, like those in the first unit.

ត	យ	ជ	ឈ
g	k	j	ch

ទ	ធ	ព	ភ
dt	t	bp	p

The consonants យ and ឈ are much less common than the others in this group.

Notice that all of these *second series* consonants can be 'matched' with a *first series* consonant of the same or similar sound from Lesson 2. Thus, in the pairs in the accompanying table, the consonant symbols are visually different but have the same sound, while the same vowel symbol is pronounced in two different ways:

first series	*second series*	*first series*	*second series*
កា	គា	ខា	យា
gaa	gee-a	kaa	kee-a
ចា	ជា	ឆា	ឈា
jaa	jee-a	chaa	chee-a
តា	ទា	ថា	ធា
dtaa	dtee-a	taa	tee-a

Vowels

The two new vowels in this unit can be added relatively painlessly since their pronunciations remain the same with both first series and second series consonants:

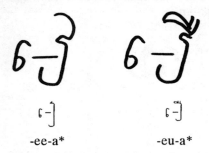

ເ−ຯ   ເ−ຯ

-ee-a*   -eu-a*

*In our transcription the 'a' changes to 'u' if there is a final consonant.

Words with no written vowel 🔲

Many Khmer words consist of simply two consonants, with no vowel symbol appearing, e.g. ជិង, មក. These words are usually pronounced with an inherent **-or** sound. Some common words with an initial *second series* consonant are, however, pronounced with an inherent **-oa** sound. Below are some examples of more common words with no written vowel.

ជង	ផង	មក	យក	រក	ពង
dorng	porng	moak	yoak	rork	bporng
'time'	'too'	'come'	'take'	'look for'	'egg'

Exercise 4 🔲

All the words in this exercise begin with the new *second series* consonants:

គិត	គូ	គោ	ជា	ជិត
ជូន	ជួប	ជួយ	ជៀន	ជៀ

ទា ទិញ ទូ ទៅ ទៀត
ទៀន ធានា ធូប ពិត ពី
ពីរ ពួក ពិព្រាក ភាត ភូមិ*

* The **-i** sound on the last syllable is not pronounced here; the spelling reflects the Sanskrit origin of the word.

Exercise 5

Some more short sentences; again, don't worry about meanings!

1 ទៅ មិនទៅ គិតមិនទៅ តាគិតមិនទៅ
2 ទូក តាមទូក ទៅតាមទូក ទៅតាមទូកពិព្រាក
3 ភូមិ ទៅភូមិ ទៅភូមិពិព្រាក ជួនកាលទៅភូមិពិព្រាក
4 រៀន មករៀន មិនមករៀន កូនមិនមករៀន

Vocabulary

ទៅ	go	ភូមិ	village
ជួនកាល	sometimes	កូន	child
គិត	think	មិន	not
តា	grandfather, old man	មក	come
ទូក	boat	រៀន	study (v)
តាមទូក	by boat		

Final consonants

So far, the words and syllables we have met have ended either in a long vowel (represented by two vowel symbols e.g. *-aa, -ao* etc. in the transcription) or in the sounds **m, n, ng, ñ, y, w** and **l**; we noted that the Cambodian equivalent of letter **r** appeared at the end of some words but was not pronounced. Cambodian, like all languages, has a limited number of sounds that can occur at the end of a syllable. The final consonant sounds in Cambodian can be represented in our transcription as:

m n ng ñ y w l k p t ch

When **k, p, t, ch** sounds occur at the end of a word they are articulated slightly differently from when they occur at the beginning. We say the sound is not 'released'. An example of an 'unreleased t' in English is the final letter in 'rat' when the words 'rat trap' are said quickly. At first you will probably feel that **k, p, t, ch** all sound the same at the end of a word; within a very short time, however, you will find you can actually hear a distinct difference between these 'unreleased' consonants.

From the list of possible final consonant sounds above, you will notice that **g, b, bp, dt,** or **j** sounds do not occur. When Cambodian letters represented by these sounds occur at the end of a word, their pronunciation changes to **k, p, p, t** and **ch** respectively.

Final consonant sound	*Cambodian letter*		
p	ប	ព	
t	ត	ទ	
k	ក	ខ	គ
ch	ច	ជ	

Exercise 6

Nearly all of the words in this exercise end with a **p, t, k,** or **ch** sound

ក្បច	ខាត	ខួច	គិត	ក្បរ	ស្ងួត
ចត	ចប	ចាក	ព្រទ	ភាគ	ភាព
ដួច	គូច	រូប	មុខ	រាគ	រាជ

4 ni-yee-ay pee-a-saa k'mai

Speaking Cambodian

In this lesson you will learn how to:

- use *can*
- say when you don't understand something
- recognise subscript consonants

Cambodians are generally surprised and pleased that westerners make the effort to learn their language. Even the clumsiest attempts to say something in Cambodian are likely to be greeted with enthusiastic praise. But don't let fulsome praise go to your head!

ni-yee-ay pee-a-saa k'mai ▣

A: Cambodian; B: visitor

A:	loak jeh ni-yee-ay pee-a-saa	លោកចេះនិយាយភាសា
	k'mai reu dtay?	ខ្មែរឬទេ?
B:	k'nyom ni-yee-ay baan	ខ្ញុំនិយាយបាន
	bon-dteuch bon-dtoo-ich.	បន្តិចបន្តួច។
A:	dtay	ទេ
	loak ni-yee-ay k'mai la-or nah.	លោកនិយាយខ្មែរល្អណាស់។
	nou s'rok k'mai yoo dtay?	នៅស្រុកខ្មែរយូរទេ?
B:	meun yoo bpon-maan dtay.	មិនយូរប៉ុន្មានទេ។
A:	loak sor-say uk-sor k'mai	លោកសរសេរអក្សរខ្មែរ

	baan dtay?	ប្រានទេ?
B:	k'nyom s'dup meun baan dtay.	ខ្ញុំស្ដាប់មិនប្រានទេ។
	soam taa m'dorng dtee-ut	
	baan dtay?	សូមថាម្ដងទៀត ប្រានទេ?
A:	baat loak sor-say uk-sor	ប្រាទ។ លោកសរសេរ អក្សរ
	k'mai baan dtay?	ខ្មែរ ប្រានទេ?
B:	'uk-sor' k'nyom s'dup meun	អក្សរ ខ្ញុំស្ដាប់មិន
	baan dtay.	ប្រានទេ ។
	pee-a-saa ong-klayh taa ay?	ភាសាអង់គ្លេសថាអ្វី?
A:	pee-a-saa ong-klayh taa 'letter'.	ភាសាអង់គ្លេសថា 'letter'។
B:	baat or-gOOn.	ប្រាទ អរគុណ។
	yoo-ul hai-ee.	យល់ហើយ។
	k'nyom sor-say k'mai	ខ្ញុំសរសេរខ្មែរ
	meun baan dtay	មិនប្រានទេ
	bon-dtai jong ree-un.	ប៉ុន្តែចង់រៀន។

A: *Do you speak Cambodian?*
B: *I can a little.*
A: *No! You speak it very well.*
Have you been in Cambodia a long time?
B: *Not very long*
A: *Can you write Cambodian?*
B: *I don't understand.*
Could you say that again, please?
A: *Yes. Can you write Cambodian?*
B: *I don't understand the word 'uksor'.*
What is it in English?
A: *It means 'letter' in English.*
B: *Yes. Thank you. I understand.*
I can't write Cambodian, but I want to learn.

Vocabulary

jeh	to know (how to do something)	ចេះ
ni-yee-ay	to speak	និយាយ
reu dtay?	*question form*	ឬទេ?
baan	to be able to, can	បាន
bon-teuch bon-dtoo-ich	a little	បន្តិចបន្តួច
la-or	well, good, beautiful	ល្អ
meun . . . bpon-maan dtay	not very . . .	មិន . . .ប៉ុន្មានទេ
sor-say	to write	សរសេរ
uk-sor	letter (of the alphabet)	អក្សរ
uk-sor k'mai	Cambodian script	អក្សរខ្មែរ
s'dup baan	to understand	ស្តាប់បាន
s'dup meun baan dtay	to not understand	ស្តាប់មិនបានទេ
soam	please	សូម
taa	to say	ថា
m'dorng	one time	ម្តង
dtee-ut	extra, further	ទៀត
or-gOOn	thank you	អរគុណ
yoo-ul	to understand	យល់
jong	to want to	ចង់

Language points

. . . reu dtay? *questions*

Questions that end in **. . . reu dtay?** are similar to those that end in **. . . dtay** (see Lesson 3) and can be answered in the same way; while **. . . reu dtay?** can be literally translated as '. . .or not?', it is not as abrupt as the English.

baan *(i)*

The Cambodian word for 'can', 'able to' is **baan**. It comes at the end of a sentence, after the main verb:

k'nyom sor-say uk-sor k'mai baan.

ខ្ញុំសរសេរ អក្សរខ្មែរ បាន។

I *can* write Cambodian.

In negative sentences **baan** is 'sandwiched' in the middle of the negative expression **meun ... dtay** at the end of the sentence:

k'nyom ni-yee-ay k'mai *meun* baan dtay.

ខ្ញុំនិយាយខ្មែរមិនបានទេ។

I *can't* speak Cambodian.

If an adverb is used (e.g. I can speak Cambodian *well/a little/ fluently* etc.) it occurs after the word **baan**.

goa-ut sor-say uk-sor k'mai baan *la-or*.

គាត់សរសេរ អក្សរខ្មែរ បានល្អ។

He writes Cambodian *nicely*.

loak ni-yee-ay baan *ch'bah* ('clear').

លោកនិយាយ បានច្បាស់។

You speak *clearly*.

k'nyom ni-yee-ay baan bon-dteuch bon-dtoo-ich.

ខ្ញុំនិយាយ បានបន្តិចបន្តួច។

I speak *a little*.

'Not very . . .'

In Lesson 3 you met the question word **. . . bpon-maan?** ('how many?'). When **bpon-maan** occurs in the pattern **meun . . . bpon-maan dtay** it means 'not very . . .' or 'hardly . . .':

meun t'lai bpon-maan dtay
not very expensive

មិនថ្លៃប៉ុន្មានទេ

meun tom bpon-maan dtay
not very big

មិនធំប៉ុន្មានទេ

meun la-or bpon-maan dtay
not very good

មិនល្អប៉ុន្មានទេ

m'dorng dtee-ut

In Lesson 3 we noted that the word **moo-ay** ('one') contracted to **m'** when followed by a classifier (e.g. **m'nay-uk** 'one person'). **m'dorng** is a contraction of **moo-ay** + **dorng** ('time'); **dtee-ut** means 'additional', 'extra'.

'Understand'

In the conversation two different words are used for 'understand' – **s'dup baan** and **yoo-ul**. The learner can use both to say 'I don't understand'. There are, however, situations where the two expressions are not interchangeable. **s'dup** actually means 'listen', so a Cambodian pupil puzzling alone over complicated mathematical equations might mutter to himself **'meun yoo-ul dtay'**.

Exercise 1

How would you answer if a Cambodian asked you these questions?

1 jeh ni-yee-ay pee-a-saa
k'mai reu dtay? ចេះនិយាយភាសា
ខ្មែរឬទេ?

2 ree-un pee-a-saa k'mai nou ee-naa? រៀនភាសាខ្មែរ
នៅឯណា ?

3 ree-un pee-a-saa k'mai yoo dtay រៀនភាសាខ្មែរយូរទេ?

4 nay-uk naa bong-ree-un ('teach')
loak? អ្នកណាបង្រៀន
លោក ?

5 pee-a-saa k'mai bpi-baak
('difficult') dtay? ភាសាខ្មែរពិបាកទេ?

6 sor-say uk-sor k'mai baan dtay? សរសេរអក្សរខ្មែរ
បានទេ?

Exercise 2

Substitute the given word in the appropriate place in the sentence. Keep each substitution until it has to be replaced so that each sentence moves further away from the original.

1 k'nyom ni-yee-ay pee-a-saa baa-rung ខ្ញុំនិយាយភាសាប៉ារ៉ាំង ('French') baan bon-dteuch bon-dtoo-ich.

ប៉ានបន្តិចបន្តុច ៤

2 borng bproh បងប្រុស

3 ong-klayh អង់គ្លេស

4 la-or ល្អ

5 sor-say សរសេរ

6 s'roo-ul ('easy') ស្រួល

7 merl aan ('to read') មើលអាន

8 m'dai k'nyom ម្ដាយខ្ញុំ

Exercise 3

How would you say the following in Cambodian?

1 Do you speak English?
2 I don't speak French.
3 Do you understand?
4 Please say that again.
5 I can speak a little Cambodian but I can't write it.

ree-un pee-a-saa k'mai
Learning Cambodian

Vocabulary

mOOn	before	មុន
dtrou	have to, must	ត្រូវ
saa-laa ree-un	school	សាលារៀន
dail	which, where	ដែល
bong-ree-un	to teach	បង្រៀន
t'ngai	day	ថ្ងៃ

maong	hour	ម៉ោង
merl aan	to read	មើលអាន
sor-say	to write	សរសេរ
kroo	teacher	គ្រូ
gom-bpoo-ung tom	Kompong Tom	កំពង់ធំ
mOOn dom-boang	at first	មុនដំបូង
s'roo-ul	easy	ស្រួល
bpi-baak	difficult	ពិបាក
bpee bay	two or three; a few	ពីរបី
kai	month	ខែ
yoo-ul taa	think(s) that	យល់ថា

mOOn dtou t'wer gaa nou s'rok k'mai

មុនទៅធ្វើការនៅស្រុកខ្មែរ

Sally dtrou ree-un pee-a-saa k'mai. nou

Sally ត្រូវរៀនភាសាខ្មែរ។ នៅ

s'rok nih mee-un dtai saa-laa ree-un

ស្រុកនេះមានតែសាលារៀន

moo-ay dail gay bong-ree-un pee-a-saa

មួយដែលគេបង្រៀនភាសា

k'mai. Sally dtou saa-laa nih

ខ្មែរ។ Sally ទៅសាលានេះ

moo-ay t'ngai bpee maong. ree-un

មួយថ្ងៃពីរម៉ោង។ រៀន

ni-yee-ay, merl aan neung sor-say

និយាយ មើលអាន នឹងសរសេរ

uk-sor k'mai. kroo bong-ree-un jee-a

អក្សរខ្មែរ។ គ្រូបង្រៀនជា

k'mai. moak bpee kait gom-bpoo-ung tom

ខ្មែរ ។ មកពីខេត្តកំពង់ធំ

bpon-dtai nou s'rok nih yoo hai-ee. mOOn

ប៉ុន្តែនៅស្រុកនេះយូរ ហើយ ។ មុន

dom-boang pee-a-saa k'mai meun s'roo-ul

ដំបូងភាសាខ្មែរមិនស្រួល

ree-un dtay. Sally s'dup kroo meun baan

រៀនទេ ។ Sally ស្ដាប់គ្រូមិនបាន

dtay. bpi-baak ni-yee-ay. bpon-dtai

ទេ ។ ពិបាកនិយាយ ។ ប៉ុន្តែ

grao-ee bpee ree-un baan bpee bay kai

ក្រោយពីរៀនបានពីរបីខែ

hai-ee Sally ni-yee-ay baan la-or,

ហើយ Sally និយាយបានល្អ

merl baan s'roo-ul neung sor-say baan

មើលបានស្រួល និង សរសេរបាន

bon-dteuch bon-dtoo-ich. ay-lou nih

បន្តិចបន្តួច ។ ឥឡូវនេះ

Sally yoo-ul taa pee-a-saa k'mai

Sally យល់ថាភាសាខ្មែរ

meun bpi-baak bpon-maan dtay.

មិនពិបាកប៉ុន្មានទេ ។

Script

Consonant clusters and subscript

When two consonant sounds occur together at the beginning of a word – e.g. **t'wer**, **s'ray**, **kroo**, etc. – the second consonant symbol is written underneath the initial consonant. Each consonant symbol in

Cambodian has in addition to its normal form a *subscript* form. Thus, for every consonant symbol, it is also necessary to learn a subscript form. In some cases the subscript consonants are very similar to their 'parent' consonants; in other instances there is virtually no resemblance whatsoever.

In this lesson we shall go back to the consonants from Lesson 1 and learn their subscript forms. Just as the consonants in Lesson 1 were the most common letters in Cambodian, so, too, their subscript forms are the most common. All of these consonants, remember, are *second series* consonants.

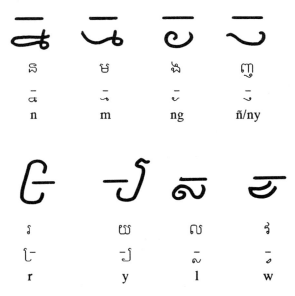

Consonant clusters and vowels

If the initial consonant and subscript consonant both belong to the same series, then the vowel will take that series.

ត្រូ	ជ្រូក	ទ្វារ
kroo*	ch'rook	t'wee-a

But if an initial consonant belonging to the first series is followed by one of the subscript consonants above, then the vowel takes the first series pronunciation.

ឆ្នាំ	ខ្លា	ក្នុង
ch'num	klaa	k'nong

* Note that a number of initial consonants change their pronunciation in a cluster. Thus, for example, ក and គ normally change from **g** to **k**, while ច and ជ change from **j** to **ch**.

Consonants

All of the new consonants in this lesson are *first series* consonants.

ណ ស ហ ឡ អ

ណ	ស	ហ	ឡ	អ
n	s	h	l	zero consonant

Khmer words never end with an **-s** sound, although the letter ស occurs at the end of many words. In such cases the preceding vowel is pronounced with marked aspiration at the end, which is represented in the transcription by **-h**.

ចាស	មាស
jaah	mee-ah

'Zero consonant'

When we have learned vowel symbols, a dash has been used to represent the position of the consonant in relation to the vowel symbol. When a word begins with a vowel sound, a consonant symbol still has to be substituted in the appropriate position. Thus a word that begins with an **-aa** sound cannot simply start with the letter ា because, as we have already seen, this letter must always follow a consonant. The 'zero consonant' serves this function, producing no sound of its own when it occurs with a written vowel symbol.

អាន	អាយុ
aan	aayOO

Exercise 4

See how many examples of the new consonants and subscript consonants you can find in the passage below:

ខ្ញុំឈ្មោះ គាន់ យុន ស្រុកកំណើតនៅវរកាកោង ដែលស្ថិត
នៅតាមដងទន្លេ មេកុង មានចម្ងាយ ១៨ គីឡូម៉ែត្រពី
ក្រុងភ្នំពេញ ។ ឪពុកខ្ញុំឈ្មោះ គាន់ ម៉ូរ ម្ដាយឈ្មោះ
នាងសុខគី ជាអ្នករកស៊ីធ្វើចំការ ។ គាត់មានដីជា
ច្រើនហិកតាសំរាប់ធ្វើដំណាំ តាមរដូវ ។ តែនៅឆ្នាំ
១៩៦៥ គាត់លក់ចំការ ចោលរួចបើកហាងលក់របស់
ផ្សេង ៗ នៅផ្សារវរកាកោង ។ ខ្ញុំមានបងប្រុសម្នួយ
និងបងស្រីម្ដួយ ខ្ញុំជាកូនពៅ ឪពុកម្ដាយខ្ញុំនឹងបង ៗ
ចូលចិត្តហៅខ្ញុំ 'អាពៅ' ។ យើងខ្ញុំបងប្អូនទាំងបីនាក់
រស់នៅយ៉ាងសុខសប្បាយ តាំងពីក្មេងដល់ធំ ក្រោម
ការថែរក្សាយ៉ាងយកចិត្តទុកដាក់របស់ឪពុកម្ដាយ ។
នៅឆ្នាំ ១៩៦៨ ខ្ញុំបានរៀនចប់មធ្យមសិក្សាទី ២ ថ្នាក់
ចុងបំផុតព្រមទាំង ប្រឡងជាប់ 'បាស្ ទី ២' នៅ
វិទ្យាល័យស៊ីសុវត្ថិក្រុងភ្នំពេញ ។ តាមបំណងរបស់ខ្ញុំ ខ្ញុំនឹង
បន្តការសិក្សានៅមហាវិទ្យាល័យវេជ្ជពេទ្យនៅដើម
ឆ្នាំ ១៩៧០ ខាងមុខនោះ ប៉ុន្តែអភ័ព្វពេកណាស់ នៅថ្ងៃទី
១៨ មីនា ១៩៧០ស្រាប់តែកើតមានរដ្ឋប្រហារ ដឹកនាំដោយ
លោកឧដ្ឋមសេនីលន់នល់ ។

Exercise 5

Here are some common words beginning with the new consonants:

| ណា | ណាយ | សាប | សុខ | ស្ូម |

សូន	សង	សៀម	ហា	ហាង
ហុកសិប	ហ្ឫរ	ហ្មុស	ហៅ	ឡាន
អាច*	អាយុ	អាកាស	អាគារ	សាលា†

* If you have the tape, you will notice that the vowel changes to an -ai sound when the final consonant is ច.

† Irregular pronunciation: **saa-laa** (not 'saa-lee-a').

Exercise 6

The words in this exercise all begin with a consonant cluster. In each case check the series of the initial consonant. Remember, if the initial consonant is first series, then the vowel will be first series pronunciation also.

ក្តា	ក្តាន	ត្រា	ក្រសារ	ថ្មី
ជ្រាប	ជ្រុង	ទ្វារ	ព្រម	ស្មួល
ព្រុយ	ក្មុយ	ក្មុង	ខ្លា	ខ្លាច
ខ្លុន	ឃ្លាន	ឆ្លាយ	ឆ្លា	ឆ្លា

Exercise 7

Now try these short sentences. Try to work out what they mean using the vocabulary given; you already know several of the words used.

1 រៀន សាលារៀន មកសាលារៀន ក្រុមកសាលារៀន
2 យួរ ព្រុយយួរ តាព្រុយយួរ តាសុខព្រុយយួរ
3 មក ព្រមមក មិនព្រមមក ក្រុសារមិនព្រមមក

Vocabulary

ព្រុយ	to be sad	ព្រម	to agree
តា	old man, grandfather	ក្រុសារ	family
សុខ	Sok (personal name)		

5 ree-un saa jee-a t'may

Review

A lot of ground has been covered in the first four lessons. Already you are able to say quite a few things about yourself and to engage in simple small talk. You have also made substantial progress in mastering the Cambodian alphabet.

The aim of this unit is to give you a chance to test yourself on how well you are absorbing Cambodian. If you find that you are having some difficulties with the test exercises in this unit, go back and work through the first four units again.

Exercise 1

How would you say the following in Cambodian:

1 What's your name? លោកឈ្មោះ អ្វី?

2 What's your family name? ឈ្មោះ ត្រកូល អ្វី?

3 Where do you come from? លោកមកពីណា?

4 What country do you come from? មកពីស្រុក អ្វី?

or more colloquially មកពីស្រុកណា?

5 What province do you come from? មកពីខេត្ត អ្វី?

or more colloquially មកពីខេត្តណា?

6 What (job) do you do? ធ្វើការ អ្វី?

7 Where do you work? ធ្វើការ នៅឯណា?

8 Have you worked there for a long time?

ធ្វើការនៅឯនោះយូរ ទេ?

9 Are you married? ការហេីយបុនៅ?

10 What does your husband do? ប្ដីធ្វេីការ អ្វី?

11 Does your wife work? ប្រពន្ធធ្វេីការទេ?

12 How many years have you been married?

ការបុ៉ន្មានឆ្នាំហេីយ?

13 Do you have any children? មានកូនហេីយបុនៅ?

14 How many children do you have? មានកូនបុ៉ន្មាននាក់?

15 How many sons do you have? មានកូនប្រុសបុ៉ន្មាននាក់?

16 How old are you? លោកអាយុ បុ៉ន្មាន?

17 How old is your husband? ប្ដីអាយុ បុ៉ន្មាន?

18 How old is your eldest son? កូនប្រុសទីមួយអាយុ បុ៉ន្មាន?

19 Do you have any brothers and sisters?

មានបងប្អូនទេ?

20 Does your sister have any children?

បងស្រីមានកូនហេីយបុនៅ?

21 Do you speak Cambodian? ចេះនិយាយភាសាខ្មែរបុទេ?

22 You speak English very well. លោកនិយាយភាសាអង់គ្លេស
 បានល្អ។

23 I speak a little Cambodian. ខ្ញុំនិយាយភាសាខ្មែរ បានបន្តិច
បន្ដច។

24 Have you studied English a long time?

រៀនភាសាអង់គ្លេសយូរទេ?

25 Who teaches English? អ្នកណាបង្រៀនភាសា
អង់គ្លេស?

26 Where does your teacher come from?

គ្រូលោកមកពីណា?

Exercise 2

Read the following Cambodian words:

នៅ	មិន	យួរ	ប្បាន	ទៅ
រៀន	អាយុ	ឆ្នាំ	នាង	លុយ
បី	ប្បាយ	ជាង	ពីរ	គ្មាន
ព្រាំ	មាន	មួយ	ប៊ុន	កូន
មក	សូម	ក្នុង	លា	និយាយ
តាម	គិត	ដង	ហាង	ស្រួល
ខ្លាច	ហៅ	ឃ្លាន	ភូមិ	ថ្មី
ពិព្បាក	គូច	ភាគ	ពួក	គ្រូ

6 jih see-kloa

Taking a cyclo

In this lesson you will learn about:

- bargaining with cyclo drivers
- numbers 21–100
- independent vowel symbols

The easiest way to get around in Phnom Penh is to take a 'cyclo' – the local pedicab. Before sitting down, make sure that the cyclo driver has understood where it is you want to go and that you have agreed on the price. Find out about prices beforehand and try to bargain with the driver, but keep your 'haggling' brief and polite, and expect even then to pay more than locals. At present many moped owners offer their own private 'taxi service'. Until you feel confident about finding your way around, it is probably best to stick to the conventional 'cyclo'.

To summon a cyclo, raise your hand and with the palm facing downwards, signal to the driver with a downwards beckoning motion.

In our conversation below, Frank is being ultra-cautious in asking the cyclo driver if he knows the New Market, since it is a place that every Phnom Penh inhabitant would know. On the other hand, cyclo driving is a common occupation for newcomers to Phnom Penh migrating from rural areas in search of a better living in the capital.

jih see-kloa ▢▢

A: Frank; B: cyclo driver

A: p'saa t'may s'koa-ul dtay?   ផ្សារថ្មីស្គាល់ទេ?

B: baat s'koa-ul.   ប្រាទ ស្គាល់។

A: dtou t'lai bpon-maan?   ទៅថ្លៃប៉ុន្មាន?

B: m'roy ree-ul.   មួយរយរៀល។

A: oa, t'lai nah   អូ ថ្លៃណាស់

    haa seup ree-ul baan dtay?   ហាសិបរៀលបានទេ?

B: meun baan dtay.   មិនបានទេ។

    p'saa t'may ch'ngai   ផ្សារថ្មីឆ្ងាយ

    m'roy ree-ul meun t'lai dtay.   មួយរយរៀលមិនថ្លៃទេ។

A: meun ch'ngai bpon-maan dtay.   មិនឆ្ងាយប៉ុន្មានទេ។

    toa-um-ma-daa k'nyom dtou p'saa   ធម្មតាខ្ញុំទៅផ្សារ

    t'may dtai haa seup ree-ul dtay.   ថ្មីតែហាសិបរៀលទេ។

B: bpait seup ree-ul joh.   ប៉ែតសិបរៀលចុះ។

A: joh jeut seup ree-ul baan dtay?   ចុះ ចិតសិបរៀលបានទេ?

B: baan.   បាន។

A: *Do you know the New Market?*
B: *Yes.*
A: *How much to go (there)?*

B: *A hundred riels*
A: *Oh, that's expensive.*
Can you go for 50 riels?
B: *No, I can't. The New Market is a long way.*
A hundred riels isn't expensive.
A: *It's not very far.*
Usually I go to the New Market for
only fifty riels.
B: *Eighty riels, then.*
A: *How about seventy riels?*
B: *All right.*

Useful expressions 📼

Turn left.
bot dtou kaang ch'wayng. បត់ទៅខាងឆ្វេង។

Turn right.
bot dtou kaang s'dum. បត់ទៅខាងស្ដាំ។

Go straight on.
dtou mOOk dtrong. ទៅមុខត្រង់។

Stop here.
chOOp dtrong neung hai-ee. ឈប់ត្រង់ហ្នឹងហើយ។

Please take me to . . .
soam joon k'nyom dtou . . . សូមជូនខ្ញុំទៅ . . .

Vocabulary

p'saa t'may	New Market	ផ្សារថ្មី
s'koa-ul	to know (people, places)	ស្គាល់
t'lai	price; expensive	ថ្លៃ
t'lai bpon-maan?	how much does it cost?	ថ្លៃប៉ុន្មាន?
ch'ngai	far	ឆ្ងាយ
m'roy (moo-ay + roy)	one hundred	មួយរយ
ree-ul	riel (unit of currency)	រៀល
oa	*exclamation*	អូ
haa seup	fifty	ហាសិប

toa-um-ma-daa	usually	ធម្មតា
dtai . . . dtay	only	តែ . . . ទេ
bpait seup	eighty	ប៉ែតសិប
jeut seup	seventy	ចិតសិប
joh	. . . then; how about . . .?	ចុះ
bot	to turn	បត់
kaang	side	ខាង
ch'wayng	left	ឆ្វេង
s'dum	right	ស្ដាំ
mOOk	front	មុខ
dtrong	straight	ត្រង់
chOOp	to stop	ឈប់
dtrong neung	right here	ត្រង់ហ្នឹង
joon	to take, lead	ជូន

Language points

'Know'

In Lesson 4 you met the verb **jeh** which meant 'to know a language'. The word **s'koa-ul** means 'to know' in the sense of being acquainted with a person or a place. The two words are not interchangeable. 'Know', in the sense of knowing a fact, is **deung** and the normal way of saying 'I don't know' is **meun deung dtay**.

loak *jeh* ong-klayh dtay?　លោកចេះអង់គ្លេសទេ?
Do you *speak* English?

loak *s'koa-ul* loak Sok dtay?　លោកស្គាល់លោកសុខទេ?
Do you *know* Mr Sok?

loak Sok gaa hai-ee mairn dtay?　លោកសុខការហើយ
Mr Sok is married, isn't he?　មែនទេ?

I don't know.

Numbers 21–100

twenty-one	**m'pay moo-ay**	ម្ភៃមួយ	២១
twenty-two	**m'pay bpee**	ម្ភៃពីរ	២២
twenty-three	**m'pay bay**	ម្ភៃបី	២៣
twenty-four	**m'pay boo-un**	ម្ភៃបួន	២៤
thirty	**saam seup**	សាមសិប	៣០
thirty-one	**saam seup moo-ay**	សាមសិបមួយ	៣១
thirty-two	**saam seup bpee**	សាមសិបពីរ	៣២
forty	**sai seup**	សែសិប	៤០
fifty	**haa seup**	ហាសិប	៥០
sixty	**hok seup**	ហុកសិប	៦០
seventy	**jeut seup**	ចិតសិប	៧០
eighty	**bpait seup**	ប៉ែតសិប	៨០
ninety	**gao seup**	កៅសិប	៩០
hundred	**(moo-ay) roy**	(មួយ)រយ	១០០

dtai . . . dtay

The basic meaning of **dtai** is 'but'. When it occurs before a noun and is followed by **dtay** it means 'only':

> **k'nyom mee-un *dtai* m'roy ree-ul dtay.**
> ខ្ញុំមានតែមួយរយរៀលទេ។
> I have got *only* 100 riels.

joh

joh occurs twice in the dialogue, first at the end of a sentence when the cyclo driver has lowered the price to 80 riels and then immediately afterwards when B suggests a price of 70 riels. The second usage is perhaps the more common, where **joh** can be translated as 'how about . . .?'

Exercise 1   🔲

Below are some well-known places in Phnom Penh. Practise asking a cyclo driver the fare to these places. Use the pattern:

dtou ... t'lai bpon-maan?   ទៅ ... ថ្លៃប៉ុន្មាន?

1	Wat Phnom	woa-ut p'nOOm	វត្តភ្នំ
2	Manorom Hotel	son-taa-gee-a ma-noa-rom	សណ្ឋាគារមនោរម្យ
3	O Russei Market	p'saa oa-reu-say	ផ្សារ អូឫស្សី
4	New Market	p'saa t'may	ផ្សារ ថ្មី
5	Olympic Stadium	staad oa-lum-bpeek	ស្តាត អូឡាំពិក

Exercise 2

How would you say:

1 Do you know the Olympic Stadium?
2 How much to go to the Manorom Hotel?
3 One hundred riels is very expensive.
4 It's not very far.
5 How about eighty riels?

Exercise 3   🔲

This exercise is to test your bargaining powers! Some cyclo drivers quote you the fares below. Tell them it is expensive and that normally you go for half that amount. The first one is done for you.

1	A:	**m'roy ree-ul.**	មួយរយរៀល។
	B:	**t'lai nah.**	ថ្លៃណាស់។
		toa-um-ma-daa k'nyom dtou	ធម្មតាខ្ញុំទៅ
		dtai haa seup ree-ul dtay.	តែហាសិបរៀលទេ។
2		**bpait seup ree-ul**	ប៉ែតសិបរៀល
3		**hok seup ree-ul**	ហកសិបរៀល

Script

Subscript consonants

Here are the subscript forms for the *first series* consonants you learned in Lesson 2:

ក	ខ	ច	ឆ	ដ
្ក	្ខ	្ច	្ឆ	្ដ
g	k	j	ch	d

ត	ថ	ប	ផ
្ត	្ថ	្ប	្ផ
dt	t	b	p

The vowel following these subscript consonants will always be pronounced with *first series* value, even if the initial consonant belongs to the *second series*:

ម្ដាយ   ល្បី

m'dai   **l'bay**

Vowels

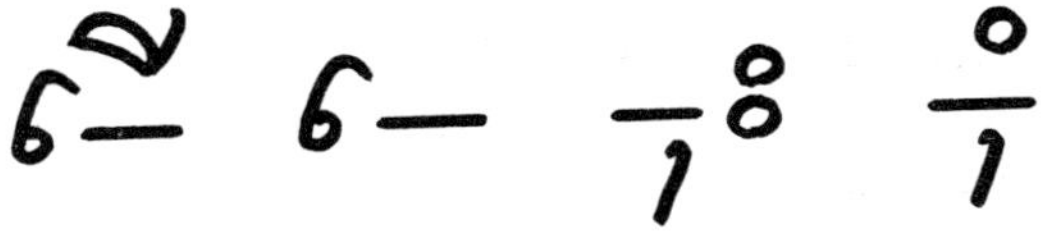

	ើ-	េ-*	-ុះ	-ុំ
(first series)	-ar	-ay	-oh	-om
(second series)	-er	-ay	-OOh	-OOm

* For the sake of simplicity, the vowel េ- is transcribed the same way for both *first* and *second series* although there is a slight difference in pronunciation. In the *first series* the vowel moves from an **-ay** sound towards an **-ee** sound, whereas in the *second series* it remains constant.

It is pronounced completely differently when it is followed by one of the following letters: ច, ឆ, ជ, ឈ, ញ. In such cases it is normally pronounced with an **-eu** sound.

Independent vowel symbols (i)

In Lesson 4 we saw how the 'zero consonant' was used to write words that begin with a vowel sound, like **aa-gaah** and **aa-yOO**. Unfortunately that is not the whole story. There are some words in Cambodian which begin with a vowel sound, but instead of being written with 'zero consonant' they are written with special 'independent' (because they do not appear on top of or underneath a consonant) vowel symbols. Some appear in very common words – others you may never come across. In this lesson we shall be concerned with just two of these symbols:

ឌ   ឱ្

ឌ   ឱ្

ai   oa

e.g. ឌណា?   e.g. ឱ្ពុក

ai-naa? ('where?')   oa-bpOOk ('father')

Exercise 4

This exercise provides practice in reading the new *first series* subscript consonants.

ផ្កា	ឆ្កត	ស្ករ	ម្កាង	ឡ្មេន
ខ្ចី	ប៉ុន្ម	ប្លរ	ផ្កាស	ម្កាយ
ស្លាយ	ស្លា	ស្លាន	ស្ថិត	ក្បាល
ច្បារ	ស្កាញ	ក្បិត	ក្បុង	ល្បី

Exercise 5

This exercise gives you a chance to practise reading the new vowels, first with a single initial consonant and then with an initial consonant cluster.

បើ	ដើរ	ឡើង	លើ	យើង
មើល	ចេក	ដេក	ដេរ	គេ
កេង	លេង	ពេល	ចុះ	លុះ
ផ្ដើម	ច្រើន	ប្រើ	ស្រុក	ខ្ពុ

Exercise 6 ▮▮

Now try reading this short conversation!

A: លោកទៅណា?

B: ខ្ញុំទៅធ្វើការ ។

A: ធ្វើការនៅឯណា ?

B: ធ្វើការនៅសាលារៀន ។ ខ្ញុំជាគ្រូ ។

A: សាលារៀននៅឯណា ?

B: សាលារៀននៅជិត(near)ស្ថានអូឡាំពីក ។

A: លោកបង្រៀនអ្វី?

B: បង្រៀនភាសាចិន ។

A: ភាសាចិនពិបាកទេ ?

B: ភាសាចិនពិបាកសរសេរ តែស្រួលនិយាយ ។

7 nou k'nong poa-ja-nee-ya-taan (1)

In the restaurant (1)

In this lesson you will learn about:
- ordering in a restaurant
- **hai-ee reu nou?** questions
- some diacritics

The colloquial word for restaurant is **haang bai** or 'food shop'. A more formal word, used for larger restaurants, is **poa-ja-nee-ya-taan**. Food is cheap in Cambodia and the larger restaurants offer a variety of local, Chinese and western dishes. Usually the menu will list foods in French, English and Cambodian. In Phnom Penh's 'dancing restaurants' there will be a live band and girls can be hired as dancing partners. Customers are usually there for the dancing rather than the food. Cambodian food itself is rather less spicy than Thai food. Typically a meal will consist of rice with a number of side dishes consisting of soups, salads and stir-fried dishes. In the conversation, one of the popular Cambodian dishes Sophiap orders is **som-lor m'joo** which is a sour soup made from a mixture of tomatoes, cucumbers and pineapples cooked with basil and tamarind juice.

nou k'nong poa-ja-nee-ya-taan (1) 🔲

A: waiter; B: Sophiap; C: Sally; D: Sokha

A: loak hao m'hoap hai-ee reu nou?

លោកហៅម្ហូបហើយឬនៅ?

B:	meun dtoa-un dtay.	មិនទាន់ទេ។
	soam yoak dtaa-raang m'hoap	សូមយកតារាងម្ហូប
	moak merl.	មកមើល។
D:	Sally joal jeut m'houp ay?	Sally ចូលចិត្តម្ហូបអី?
	bpi-saa m'houp heul baan dtay?	ពិសារម្ហូបហឹរ បានទេ?
C:	jaa n'yum baan.	ថា ញុាំបាន ។
B:	bar uñ-jeung soam yoak	បើអញ្ជឹងសូមយក
	som-lor m'joo dtray moo-ay jaan	សម្លម្ជូរត្រីមួយចាន
	som-lor gor-goa moo-ay jaan.	សម្លកកូរមួយចាន។
C:	chaa bong-gorng gor ch'nguñ dai.	ឆាបង្កង ក៏ឆ្ងាញ់ដែរ
B:	la-or soam yoak k'nyom	ល្អ សូមយកខ្ញុំ
	chaa bong-gorng moo-ay jaan dai	ឆាបង្កងមួយចានដែរ
	hai-ee neung bai dai.	ហើយនឹងបាយដែរ ។
A:	baat loak bpi-saa dteuk ay?	បាទ លោកពិសារទឹកអ្វី?
B:	k'nyom jong baan goa-gaa goa-laa	ខ្ញុំចង់បានកូកា-កូឡា
	moo-ay dorp hai-ee neung bee-a	មួយដប ហើយនឹងបៀរ
	moo-ay dorp dai.	មួយដបដែរ ។

A: *Have you ordered yet?*
B: *Not yet. Could I have the menu, please?*
D: *What would you like to eat, Sally?*
   Can you eat spicy food?
C: *Yes, I can.*
B: *In that case please bring one dish of **som-lor ma-joo** with fish and one dish of **som-lor gor-goa**.*
C: *The fried lobster is tasty, too.*
B: *Good. Please bring a plate of fried lobster, too, and rice.*
A: *Yes. What would you like to drink?*
B: *I'd like a bottle of Coca-Cola and a beer.*

Vocabulary

haang bai	restaurant	ហាងបាយ
poa-ja-nee-ya-taan	restaurant	ភោជនីយដ្ឋាន
hao	to call	ហៅ
m'hoap	food	ម្ហូប
hao m'hoap	to order food	ហៅម្ហូប
. . . hai-ee reu nou?	. . . yet (or not)?	ហើយឬនៅ?
meun dtoa-un dtay	not yet	មិនទាន់ទេ
yoak	to bring	យក
merl	to look at	មើល
dtaa-raang m'hoap	menu	តារាងម្ហូប
joal-jeut	to like	ចូលចិត្ត
bpi-saa	to eat	ពិសារ
heul	hot, spicy	ហឹរ
n'yum	to eat	ញ៉ាំ
som-lor	soup, stew (n)	សម្ល
som-lor gor-goa	(Cambodian dish)	សម្លកកូរ
som-lor ma-joo	(Cambodian dish)	សម្លម្ជូ
dtray	fish	ត្រី
chaa	to fry	ឆា
bong-gorng	prawn, shrimp	បង្គង
jaan	plate	ចាន
ch'nguñ	tasty	ឆ្ងាញ់
gor . . . dai	. . . too	ក៏ . . . ដែរ
dteuk	water, drink (n)	ទឹក
dorp	bottle	ដប
goa-gaa goa-laa	Coca-Cola	កូកា-កូឡា
bee-a	beer	បៀរ

Language points

baan *(ii)*

In Lesson 4 you met the word **baan** which, when it comes after the main verb and at the end of a sentence, means 'can'. But when **baan** occurs before a noun, it means 'get'. The expression **k'nyom jong baan** . . . literally means 'I want to get . . .'; while such a literal translation sounds rather abrupt, it is an acceptable expression to use when ordering food or drink.

. . . hai-ee reu nou? *questions*

The question form **. . . hai-ee reu nou?** occurs at the end of a sentence and basically means ' . . . yet (or not)?' The word **reu** is often dropped in fast speech.

To say 'yes' to a **hai-ee reu nou?** question, repeat the main verb and add **hai-ee**.

A 'no' answer to this question is simply **meun dtoa-un dtay**:

loak hao m'hoap *hai-ee reu nou?* លោកហៅម្ហូបហើយឬនៅ?
Have you ordered *yet?*
meun dtoa-un dtay. មិនទាន់ទេ។
No.

loak n'yum bai *hai-ee reu nou?* លោកញ៉ាំបាយហើយឬនៅ?
Have you eaten *yet?*
n'yum hai-ee. – ញ៉ាំហើយ ។
Yes.

Cambodians commonly use this question form when asking if someone is married and if they have any children:

goa-ut gaa *hai-ee reu nou?* គាត់ការ ហើយឬនៅ?
Is she married (*yet*)?

goa-ut mee-un goan *hai-ee reu nou?* គាត់មានកូនហើយឬនៅ?
Do they have any children (*yet*)?

'Eat'

There are several words in Cambodian for 'eat':

bpi-saa polite, formal word ពិសារ

n'yum	informal	ញ៉ាំ
hoap	rustic, but widely used during Pol Pot period	ហូប
see	used for animals; vulgar when used to refer to people	ស៊ី
chun	used for monks	ឆាន់

'Rice'

bai means 'cooked rice' and, more generally, 'food'. Often it is combined with **n'yum** or **bpi-saa** to mean 'to eat'. However, to refer to rice in its uncooked state, different words are needed:

bai	cooked rice	បាយ
s'rou	unhusked rice	ស្រូវ
ong-gor	husked rice	អង្ករ

Other important 'rice' words are:

s'rai	rice field	ស្រែ
t'wer s'rai	to do rice farming	ធ្វើស្រែ
nay-uk s'rai	rice farmer	អ្នកស្រែ

Fried rice

One of the least 'threatening ' oriental foods as far as most westerners are concerned is fried rice, or in Cambodian **bai chaa**. When ordering in a restaurant you need to specify what kind of fried rice you want. The main kinds are:

bai chaa sai-ich k'daam fried rice with crab meat	បាយឆាសាច់ក្តាម
bai chaa sai-ich bong-gee-a fried rice with shrimps	បាយឆាសាច់បង្គារ
bai chaa sai-ich moa-un fried rice with chicken	បាយឆាសាច់មាន់
bai chaa sai-ich ch'rook fried rice with pork	បាយឆាសាច់ជ្រូក

The word **sai-ich** means 'meat' or 'flesh'.

Exercise 1

If you go out for a meal with Cambodians, you are almost certain to be asked some – if not all – of these questions. How would you say 'yes' in each case?

1 bpi-saa m'hoap k'mai baan dtay?   ពិសារម្ហូបខ្មែរ បានទេ?

2 m'hoap k'mai ch'nguñ dtay?   ម្ហូបខ្មែរឆ្ងាញ់ទេ?

3 bpi-saa m'houp heul baan dtay?   ពិសារម្ហូបហ៊ីរ បានទេ?

4 joal-jeut m'hoap k'mai dtay?   ចូលចិត្តម្ហូបខ្មែរ ទេ?

5 m'hoap k'mai heul dtay?   ម្ហូបខ្មែរហ៊ីរ ទេ?

Exercise 2

How would you say:

1 I can't eat spicy food.
2 The fish stew isn't very tasty.
3 Please bring me the menu.
4 I'd like a plate of chicken fried rice and a bottle of beer.

Script

Subscript consonants

Here are the subscript forms for the *second series* consonants you learned in Lesson 3 (a full list of subscript forms appears in Lesson 9):

គ	យ	ជ	ឈ
្គ	្យ	្ឈ	្ឈ
g	k	j	ch

ฑ	ฒ	ต	ถ
dt	t	bp	p

Notice that half of this group of subscript forms closely resemble the form they take as initial consonants. The vowel following *these* *second series* subscript consonants will always be *second series*.

The rules for pronouncing the vowel after a subscript consonant can now be stated as follows:

Initial consonant	Subscript consonant	Vowel value
first series	second series (Lesson 1)	first series
first series	second series (*except* Lesson 1)	second series
second series	first series	first series

While this may sound daunting in theory, in practice you will find that in the overwhelming majority of words that have an initial consonant cluster, the subscript consonant is one of the Lesson 1 consonants, so that reading the word correctly usually involves merely (!) being able to identify the class of the initial consonant and remembering the alternative vowel pronunciations.

Vowels

(first series)	-eu	-eu	-ai	-ai
(second series)	-eu	-eu	-air	-ay-ee

Note that ◌ឺ is a longer vowel than ◌ឹ.
Notice that the *second series* pronunciation of the vowel symbol ◌ឹ is the same as the *second series* pronunciation of ◌ិ; in some books

Note that ◌ឺ is a longer vowel than ◌ឹ.

Notice that the *second series* pronunciation of the vowel symbol ◌ឹ is the same as the *second series* pronunciation of ◌ិ; in some books you will see the word នឹង ('and') written as និង rather than the more conventional នឹង.

The symbol ◌់ *(i)*

This symbol is called **bon-dtok.** It occurs on the final consonant of a word. It can influence the pronunciation of a word in a number of different ways. If the word begins with a *first series* consonant and is written with the vowel ◌ា, then the symbol has the effect of shortening the vowel sound:

ប្រាប់	ចាប់	កាន់
bprup	jup	gun

If the word begins with a *second series* consonant and is written with the vowel ◌ា, then the symbol has the effect of changing the pronunciation as follows:

If the final consonant is ក, ខ, គ, ឃ, ង, then the vowel is pronounced **-ay-uk**:

នាក់	ពាក់
nay-uk	bpay-uk

With any other final consonant, the vowel is pronounced **-oa-u**:

មាន់	ទាន់
moa-un	dtoa-un

The symbol ̈

This symbol (called **t'meuñ gon-dao** – 'rat's teeth') serves two distinct functions:

It changes the pronunciation of the consonants ប and ប្ from **b** to **bp**.

ប៉ុន្មាន	ប៉ុន្តែ្	ប៉ារី
bpon-maan	bpon-dtai	bpaa-ree

It converts the following Lesson 1 *second series* consonants into *first series* consonants: ង, ញ, ម, យ, រ :

យ៉ាង	ម៉ែត្រ	ម៉ោង	រ៉ៃ
yaang	mait	maong	rai

The symbol ៗ

This symbol indicates that the previous word is repeated or *reduplicated*. Reduplication of adjectival verbs such as 'large', 'expensive', 'beautiful' is a common feature of Cambodian:

តូច ៗ
dtoa-ich dtoa-ich

Exercise 3

Some common words using the new vowel symbols:

ទឹក	នឹង	ដឹង	គឺ
តើ	ដែល	ខ្មែរ	មែន
ដៃ	ថៃ	ថ្លៃ	ថ្ងៃ

Reading menus

The menu in a Cambodian restaurant will probably look something like this.

PLATS KAMPUCHEA	KAMPUCHEA FOODS	ម្ហូបខ្មែរ
– Salade de bœuf	– Beef salad	ឆ្នាសាច់គោ
– Salade de poisson	– Fish salad	ឆ្នាត្រី
– Salade de crevettes fraîches	– Fresh shrimps salad	ឆ្នាបង្គារ ស្រស់
– Crevettes de Koh Kong	– Ko Kong shrimps	បង្គារ កោះកុង
– Soupe de canard	– Duck soup	សម្លម្ហូរ ត្រៀងទា
– Soupe de bœuf	– Beef soup	សម្លម្ហូរ ត្រៀងសាច់គោ
– Soupe de langoustine	– River lobster soup	សម្លម្ហូរ បង្គង
VERMICELLES & RIZ	NOODLES AND RICE	មីឆា . . . មីទីក . . .
– Vermicelles sautés viande de bœuf	– Sauted noodle with beef	មីឆាសាច់គោ
– Vermicelles sautés viande de porc	–Sauted noodle with pork	មីឆាសាច់ជ្រូក
– Vermicelles sautés crevettes	– Sauted noodle with shrimps	មីឆាបង្គារ
– Vermicelles sautés au crabe	– Sauted noodle with crab	មីឆាសាច់ក្ដាម
– Vermicelles sautés au poulet	– Sauted noodle with chicken	មីឆាសាច់មាន់
– Vermicelles sautés viande de boeuf	– White noodle sauted with beef	គុយទាវសាច់គោ
– Vermicelles sautés viande de porc	– White noodle sauted with pork	គុយទាវសាច់ជ្រូក
–Soupe chinoise au poulet	– Chinese noodle soup with chicken	មីទីកសាច់មាន់
–Soupe chinoise au crabe	– Chinese noodle soup with crab	មីទីកសាច់ក្ដាម

–Soupe chinoise aux crevettes	– Chinese noodle soup with shrimps	ម៊ីទឹកសាច់បង្គា
– Riz sauté au crabe	– Fried rice with crab meat	បាយឆាសាច់ក្ដាម
– Riz sauté aux crevettes	– Fried rice with shrimps	បាយឆាបង្គា
– Riz sauté au poulet	– Fried rice with chicken	បាយឆាសាច់មាន់

By now you should be able to read a lot of the words on the menu and by matching them with the translations you can work out what some of the words mean. Scan the Cambodian script for the following words:

1 បាយឆា ('fried rice')

It will be followed by another word or group of words specifying what kind of fried rice it is.

2 ម៊ី and គុយទាវឆា ('sautéd noodles')

ម៊ី are egg noodles and គុយទាវ are white noodles. Notice that the word ឆា ('stir fry') occurs in both 'fried rice' and 'sautéd noodles'.

3 ម៊ីទឹក ('Chinese noodle soup')

The word for 'egg noodles' is followed by ទឹក ('water') to indicate noodle soup and the word or words that follow specify what kind of meat will be in the soup.

4 សាច់ ('meat')

This word is usually used before the words for 'chicken', 'pork' and 'beef'.

Exercise 4

Study the menu and work out what these words mean:

1 មាន់
2 បង្គា
3 ជ្រូក
4 គោ
5 ក្ដាម

Exercise 5

If you were eating with a friend who didn't like pork, which of these dishes should you avoid?

1 មីទីកសាច់មាន់

2 គុយទាវសាច់ជ្រូក

3 ប្ចាយឆាបង្គារ

4 មីឆាសាច់ជ្រូក

5 គុយទាវសាច់គោ

8 nou k'nong poa-ja-nee-ya-taan (2)

In the restaurant (2)

> **In this lesson you will learn about:**
> - the comparative and superlative adjectives
> - *too* . . .
> - a summary of rules for the diacritic ⁻

This lesson continues in the restaurant and provides you with the language to summon waiters, express preferences, call for the bill and check out where the toilets are.

nou k'nong poa-ja-nee-ya-taan (2) 🔳

A: Som Sok; B: Waiter; C: Sally; D: Frank

A:	bpoo, bpoo	ពូ ពូ
	soam bee-a moo-ay dtee-ut	សូមបៀរមួយទៀត
	hai-ee neung dteuk sot	ហើយនឹងទឹកសុទ្ធ
	moo-ay dorp.	មួយដប។
B:	dteuk sot meun dtra-jay-uk dtay.	ទឹកសុទ្ធមិនត្រជាក់ទេ។
	loak dtrou-gaa dteuk gork dtay?	លោកត្រូវការទឹកកកទេ?
A:	dtay k'nyom yoak goa-gaa goa-laa	ទេ ខ្ញុំយកកូកា-កូឡា
	la-or jee-ung.	ល្អជាង។
	Sally dtrou-gaa bong-aim dtay?	Sally ត្រូវការ បង្អែមទេ?

c: jaa dtay k'nyom cha-ait hai-ee. ចាំទេ ខ្ញុំឆ្អែតហើយ។

a: joh Frank meun klee-un reu dtay? ចុះ Frank មិនឃ្លានឬទេ?
bong-aim nou haang nih ch'nguñ បង្អែមនៅហាងនេះឆ្ងាញ់
jee-ung gay. ជាងគេ។

d: baat dtay k'nyom n'yum bong-aim បាទ ទេ ខ្ញុំញុំាបង្អែម
k'mai meun baan dtay. ខ្លៃរមិនបានទេ។
pa-aim bpayk. ផ្អែមពេក។

a: bar un-jeung soam geut loo-ee. បើរ អញ្ចឹងសូមគិតលុយ។
soam dtoah bong-goo-un nou ee naa?
សូមទោស បង្គន់នៅឯណា?

b: bong-goo-un s'ray nou kaang s'dum បង្គន់ស្រីនៅខាងស្ដាំ
bong-goo-un bproh nou kaang ch'wayng.
បង្គន់ប្រុសនៅខាងឆ្វេង។

a: or-gOOn. អរគុណ។

b: meun ay dtay. មិនអ្វីទេ។

a: *Waiter, waiter.*
Can I have another beer, please,
and a bottle of drinking water.

b: *The water isn't cool.*
Do you want a glass with ice?

a: *No. We'd better have a coke (instead).*
Sally, would you like some dessert?

c: *No thank you, I'm full*
a: *How about you, Frank? Aren't you hungry?*
     The desserts here are the tastiest.
d: *No thank you. I can't eat Cambodian desserts.*
     They're too sweet.
a: *In that case, could we have the bill, please.*
     Excuse me, where's the toilet?
b: *The ladies' is on the right, the men's on the left.*
a: *Thank you*
b: *Don't mention it.*

Vocabulary

bpoo	waiter	ព
dteuk sot	drinking water	ទឹកសុទ្ធ
dtra-jay-uk	cool, cold	ត្រជាក់
dteuk gork	ice	ទឹកកក
la-or jee-ung	better	ល្អជាង
bong-aim	dessert, sweet (n)	បង្អែម
cha-ait	full (of food)	ឆ្អែត
klee-un	to be hungry	ឃ្លាន
pa-aim	sweet (adj)	ផ្អែម
. . . bpayk	too . . .	. . . ពេក
geut	think, calculate	គិត
loo-ee	money	លុយ
bong-goo-un	toilet	បង្គន់
meun ay dtay	never mind, don't mention it	មិនអ្វីទេ

Language points

Calling the waiter

The appropriate way of addressing a waiter or waitress will depend on how old they are and whether they are older or younger than the person addressing them:

bpoo	To address older waiters who are middle-aged or older.	ពូ
meeng	To address older waitresses who are middle-aged or older.	មីង
oan	To address younger waiters.	អូន
nee-ung	To address younger waitresses.	នាង

Comparatives and superlatives

The comparative adjective is formed by adding the word **jee-ung** after the adjective:

la-or	good	ល្អ
la-or jee-ung	better	ល្អជាង
pa-aim	sweet	ផ្អែម
pa-aim jee-ung	sweeter	ផ្អែមជាង

The superlative is formed using **jee-ung gay** after the adjective:

| la-or jee-ung gay | best | ល្អជាងគេ |
| ch'nguñ jee-ung gay | tastiest | ឆ្ងាញ់ជាងគេ |

meun ay dtay

The normal response to **or-gOOn** ('thank you') is **meun ay dtay**. Apart from meaning 'don't mention it', this phrase can be used more generally to mean 'never mind', 'don't worry about it'.

Hungry, thirsty, full up

The full word for 'hungry' is **klee-un bai** (bai = 'rice') while **klee-un dteuk** (dteuk = 'water') means 'thirsty'. If you go out for a meal with Cambodians you are sure to be asked **klee-un dtay?** and **ch'nguñ dtay?** to which you will probably feel obliged to respond **klee-un** and **ch'nguñ**. At the end of a meal you may also be asked **cha-ait hai-ee reu nou?** to which the polite response is **cha-ait hai-ee**.

'too...'

bpayk ('too') follows the adjective:

heul bpayk	too spicy	ហឹរពេក
t'lai bpayk	too expensive	ថ្លៃពេក

Exercise 1

How would you say:

1 I'd like a bottle of beer.
2 This beer isn't cold. Do you have a cold beer?
3 Could I have another bottle of Coca Cola?
4 I can't eat it. It's too sweet.
5 Could I have the bill, please?

Exercise 2

Here are the Cambodian signs for 'Toilets', 'Ladies' and 'Gentlemen'. But which is which?

1 ប្រុស
2 បង្គន់
3 ស្ត្រី

Exercise 3

Re-arrange the sentences to make a meaningful conversation!

dtay k'nyom cha-ait hai-ee.	ទេ ខ្ញុំឆ្អែតហើយ។
bprum roy hok seup ree-ul.	ប្រាំរយហុកសិបរៀល។
bong-aim k'mai pa-aim bpayk reu dtay?	បង្អែមខ្មែរផ្អែមពេកឬទេ?
dtay ch'nguñ nah.	ទេ ឆ្ងាញ់ណាស់។
loak n'yum dtay?	លោកញ៉ាំទេ?
nee-ung nee-ung soam geut loo-ee.	នាង ៗ សូមគិតលុយ

m'hoap k'mai
Cambodian food 🔲

Vocabulary

j'rarn dtai	mostly	ច្រើនតែ
yoo-ul taa	to think (that)	យល់ថា
roo-ah jee-ut	flavour, taste	រសជាតិ
doach-neh	so, therefore	ដូច្នេះ
ai . . . weuñ	as for . . .	ឯ . . . វិញ
bpayl	when	ពេល
reu	or	ឬ
joo	sour	ជូរ

k'mai j'rarn dtai yoo-ul taa m'hoap	ខ្មែរច្រើនតែយល់ថាម្ហូប
ong-klayh k'mee-un roo-ah jee-ut	អង់គ្លេសគ្មានរសជាតិ
dtay. gay taa m'hoap k'mai ch'nguñ	ទេ។ គេថាម្ហូបខ្មែរឆ្ងាញ់
jee-ung.	ជាង។
dtai nou s'rok ong-klayh	តែនៅស្រុកអង់គ្លេស
k'mee-un poa-ja-nee-ya-taan k'mai	គ្មានភោជនីយដ្ឋានខ្មែរ
dtay. doach-neh k'mai nou	ទេ។ ដូច្នេះខ្មែរនៅ
s'rok ong-klayh joal-jeut dtou	ស្រុកអង់គ្លេសចូលចិត្តទៅ
n'yum bai nou haang bai jeun	ញ៉ាំបាយនៅហាងបាយចិន
reu haang bai tai	ឬហាងបាយថៃ ។
ai ong-klayh weuñ	ឯអង់គ្លេសវិញ
bpayl gay dtou	ពេលគេទៅ
s'rok k'mai gay j'rarn dtai	ស្រុកខ្មែរ គេច្រើនតែ
n'yum m'hoap k'mai meun baan	ញ៉ាំម្ហូបខ្មែរមិនបាន
dtay. gay taa heul bpayk reu	ទេ ។ គេថាហឹរពេកឬ
pa'aim bpayk reu joo bpayk.	ផ្អែមពេក ឬជូរពេក ។

Script

Consonant clusters and subscript

Here is the last major group of subscript forms; they are all *first series* consonants.

ណ	ស	ហ	ឡ	អ
n	s	h	l	zero

Again, notice that half of this group of subscript forms closely resemble the form they take as initial consonants.

Vowels

The vowels in this group share a visual similarity in that the symbol includes a superscript circle. This usually indicates that the vowel symbol is followed by an **m** sound.

(first series)	-om	-om	-um	-ung
(second series)	-OOm	-OOm	-oa-um	-ay-ung

Exercise 4

Here are some common words using the new vowel symbols and subscripts:

ធំ	កពត	ខំ	ភ្ន	ន
ថា	ស្ងា	ថ្មា	នា	រា
ក	ខ្ទិ	បេ្ស	តាង	ទាង
មួប	លំ	ស្ពាត		

Independent vowel symbols (ii)

ឥ   ឥ

The pronunciation of this independent vowel varies from word to word. You will meet it most commonly in this word:

ឥឡូវ (នេះ) **ay-lou (nih)**   now

The symbol ᷉ (ii)

In Lesson 7 we saw how this symbol affected the pronunciation of words written with the vowel ─ា; in this lesson we deal with syllables where there is no written vowel.

If the word begins with a *first series* consonant, then the symbol simply shortens the inherent vowel **-or** to **-o**.

ដប   ដប់

dorp   dop

If the word begins with a *second series* consonant and ends with ប, ផ, ព, ភ, ម, then the vowel is pronounced **-OO**:

លប់

lOOp

If the word begins with a *second series* consonant and ends with any consonant other than those in the last example, then the vowel is pronounced **-oo-u**:

លក់

loo-uk

Summary of rules of the symbol ់

Initial consonant (* or dominant consonant in cluster)*	-ា *vowel*	*No vowel*
first series	shortens vowel e.g. ប្រាប់ **bprup** ចាប់ **jup** កាន់ **gun**	shortens inherent vowel e.g. ដប់ **dop**
second series	If the final consonant is ក, ខ, គ, ឃ, ង, then the vowel is pronounced **-ay-uk** e.g. នាក់ **nay-uk** ពាក់ **bpay-uk**	If the word ends with ប, ផ, ព, ភ, ម, then the vowel is pronounced **-OO** e.g. លប់ **lOOp** យប់ **yOOp**
	With any other final consonant, the vowel is pronounced **-oa-u** e.g. មាន់ **moa-un** ទាល់ **dtoa-ul**	With any other final consonant, the vowel is pronounced **-oo-uk** e.g. លក់ **loo-uk** យល់ **yoo-ul**

Exercise 5 📷

So far, you have met the following words spelt with ´. Use the accompanying table to work out any words you are not sure about.

បង់ នាក់ ណាស់ ចង់ អង់គ្លេស
ម្ដាក់ ស្ដាប់ ស្ដាល់ ដប់ បត់
ត្រង់ ឈប់ (មិន)ទាន់ ឆ្លាញ់ បង្កន់
សាច់

Exercise 6 📷

To finish, try to read this mini-biography about a young man called Goy. Try to draw up a family tree for him, filling in as much information as you can.

កុយមកពីភូមិតួចនៅសៀមរាប។
ឪពុកម្ដាយជាអ្នក*ស្រែ។
មានបងប្អូនពីរនាក់ ។
បងស្រីការ៍ហើយ មានកូនបីនាក់
គឺកូនស្រីម្នួយ កូនប្រុសម្នួយ។
ប្ដីបងស្រីមកពីស្វាយរៀង។
ធ្វើគ្រូនៅសាលារៀននៅភូមិកុយ។
ប្អូនប្រុសអាយុ ដប់ប្រាំប្អូនឆ្នាំហើយ។
កាត់មិនចង់ធ្វើស្រែទេ។

* Note the irregular way that អ្នក (nay-uk) is spelt here, with the subscript consonant pronounced first. Be careful to distinguish this អ្នក from the classifier **nay-uk**, spelt នាក់, but pronounced exactly the same way.

9 dtou layng meut som-luñ

Visiting a friend

In this lesson you will learn about:

- greetings and introductions
- *why?* questions
- relative pronouns

If you are invited to a Cambodian home you should take off your shoes before entering the house. Cambodians may greet you by bowing slightly with their hands placed together in a prayer-like position in front of the face at approximately chin height. You should respond in like manner. Cambodians will show respect for older, or more senior people by trying to keep their head at a lower level when passing by or talking to them. This is obviously tricky if Granny happens to be sitting down, but an obvious attempt to bend forward or stoop a little is sufficient to demonstrate some cultural sensitivity. When seated, you should avoid pointing your feet at anyone; the common western way of sitting on a chair with legs crossed and stretched out in front appears ill-mannered to Cambodians.

dtou layng meut som-luñ 🔲

A: Sophiap; B: Frank; C: Jill

A: soo-a s'day Frank   ស្តួស្ដី Frank

    sok sop-bai jee-a dtay?   សុខសប្បាយជាទេ?

B: k'nyom sok sop-bai jee-a dtay or-gOOn

ខ្ញុំសុខសប្បាយជាទេអរគុណ

joh So-pee-up aing? ចុះសុភាពឯង?

A: k'nyom gor sok sop-bai dai. ខ្ញុំក៏សុខសប្បាយដែរ

B: k'nyom jong nai noa-um loak ខ្ញុំចង់ណែនាំលោក

ao-ee s'koa-ul bpra-bpoo-un អោយស្គាល់ប្រពន្ធ

k'nyom ch'moo-ah Jill. ខ្ញុំឈ្មោះ Jill ។

Jill jeh k'mai. Jill ចេះខ្មែរ ។

A: soo-a s'day Jill. សួស្តី Jill ។

k'nyom dtrayk-or dail baan ខ្ញុំត្រេកអរដែលបាន

s'koa-ul Jill. ស្គាល់ Jill ។

maych baan jee-a Jill jeh k'mai?

ម៉េចបានជា Jill ចេះខ្មែរ?

C: k'nyom jeh klah bproo-ah k'nyom

ខ្ញុំចេះខ្លះព្រោះខ្ញុំ

dail t'wer gaa nou jOOm-rOOm

ដែលធ្វើការនៅជុំរុំ

nou s'rok tai. នៅស្រុកថៃ ។

A: mairn reu? t'wer gaa ay? មែនឬ? ធ្វើការអ្វី?

C: k'nyom bong-ree-un pee-a-saa ខ្ញុំបង្រៀនភាសា

ong-klayh. bpayl nOOh mee-un អង់គ្លេស ។ ពេលនោះមាន

bpoo-uk-maak k'mai j'rarn gor ពួកម៉ាក់ខ្មែរច្រើនក៏

jup ree-un pee-a-saa k'mai. ចាប់រៀនភាសាខ្មែរ ។

A: bpoo-gai mairn. ពូកែមែន ។

A: *Hello, Frank. How are you?*

B: *I'm fine thank-you. How about you, Sophiap?*

A: *I'm fine, too.*

B: *I'd like to introduce you to my wife. Her name is
Jill. She speaks Cambodian.*

A: *Hello, Jill. I'm pleased to meet you. How come you speak Cambodian?*

C: *I speak a bit because I used to work in a (refugee) camp in Thailand.*

A: *Really? What did you do?*

C: *I taught English. At that time I had lots of Cambodian friends so I started to learn Cambodian.*

A: *Brilliant!*

Vocabulary

soo-a s'day	hello	ស្ួស្ដី
sok sop-bai jee-a dtay?	how are you?	សុខសប្បាយជាទេ?
k'nyom sok sop-bai jee-a dtay	I'm fine	ខ្ញុំសុខសប្បាយជាទេ
aing	you; self	ឯង
nai noa-um ao-ee s'koa-ul	to introduce	ណែនាំអោយ ... ស្គាល់
dtrayk-or	pleased, delighted	ត្រេកអរ
maych baan jee-a	why . . .?	ម៉េចបានជា ...?
klah	some, somewhat	ខ្លះ
bproo-ah	because	ព្រោះ
dail	used to	ដែល

jOOm-rOOm	(refugee) camp	ជំរំ
mairn reu?	really?	មែនឬ?
bpoo-uk-maak	friend	ពួកម៉ាក
j'rarn	many	ច្រើន
jup	to begin	ចាប់
bpoo-gai	good at, clever	ពូកែ
mairn	indeed, really	មែន

Language points

Greetings

soo-a s'day is an informal greeting used between friends. More formal is **jOOm-ree-up soo-a** (ជំរាបសួរ). Both can be used at any time of the day.

sok sop-bai jee-a dtay

You are already quite familiar with the question word **dtay?** in the question **sok sop-bai jee-a dtay?** ('How are you?'). But the answer to this question is also **sok sop-bai jee-a dtay!** In the reply, the **dtay** is not the question word (although it is pronounced and written the same way) but a particle (an untranslateable word) added for emphasis. There are many such particles in spoken Cambodian which can really be learned only by listening to and imitating native speakers.

aing

aing in the dialogue basically means 'self' and is used to emphasise the preceding noun (in this case **So-pee-up**). In English we might render the same idea by stressing the word 'you' – 'And how about *you*, Sophiap?'

relative pronoun dail

You met **dail** briefly in Lesson 4 in the sentence:

mee-un dtai saa-laa moo-ay *dail* មានតែសាលាមួយដែល
gay bong-ree-un pee-a-saa k'mai. គេបង្រៀនភាសាខ្មែរ។
There is only one school *where* they teach Cambodian.

dail can mean not only 'where' but also 'who(m)' and 'which':

kroo dail bong-ree-un k'mai គ្រូដែលបង្រៀនខ្មែរ
moak bpee p'nOOm bpeuñ. មកពីភ្នំពេញ។
The teacher who teaches Cambodian comes from Phnom Penh.

saa-laa ree-un dail yerng ree-un សាលារៀនដែលយើងរៀន
meun tom bpon-maan dtay. មិនធំប៉ុន្មានទេ ។
The school where we study is not very big.

In the expression **k'nyom dtrayk-or dail baan s'koa-ul Jill**, the word **dail** could be translated as 'that'.

why . . .?

There are a number of ways of saying 'why . . .?'.

maych baan jee-a . . .? (*colloquial*) ម៉េចបានជា . . .?
maych gor . . .? (*colloquial*) ម៉េចក៏ . . .?
hait ay baan jee-a . . .? (*formal*) ហេតុអ្វីបានជា . . .?

All of these expressions require the question to be stated in full.

maych baan jee-a meun dtou dtay? ម៉េចបានជាមិនទៅទេ?
Why aren't you going?

To ask 'why?' in response to a statement, use **hait ay?** or **bproo-ah ay?**

k'nyom jong ree-un k'mai. ខ្ញុំចង់រៀនខ្មែរ។
I want to study Cambodian.

hait ay? / bproo-ah ay? ហេតុអ្វី? / ព្រោះ អ្វី?

bproo-ah ('because') is a shortened form of **bpi-bproo-ah** (ពីព្រោះ).

dail *('used to', 'to have ever . . .')*

One function of **dail** is as a relative pronoun (see above). It is also used in front of a verb to show that the action of the verb has occurred at least once. When **meun** precedes **dail** it means 'to have never . . .':

loak *dail* **n'yum m'hoap k'mai dtay?**   លោកដែលញ៉ាំម្ហូបខ្មែរទេ?

Have you *ever* eaten Cambodian food?

dail/ meun dail.   ដែល/មិនដែល។

Yes / No.

k'nyom *meun dail* **dtou s'rok k'mai.**   ខ្ញុំមិនដែលទៅស្រុកខ្មែរ។

I have *never* been to Cambodia.

goa-ut dail bong-ree-un ong-klayh.   គាត់ដែលបង្រៀនអង់គ្លេស។

She used to teach English.

jOOm-rOOm

By the late 1980s the number of Cambodian 'displaced persons' accommodated in refugee camps inside the Thai border exceeded 300,000. The largest of these, Site 2, with a population of 152,000, was for a time the second largest Cambodian 'city' after Phnom Penh. The Thai camps were closed and their inhabitants repatriated following the Paris Peace Agreement of 1991.

Exercise 1

How would you introduce Sophiap to:

1 your older sister
2 your son
3 your friend, Mr Som Sok
4 your mother
5 your teacher

Exercise 2

Match up the questions and answers below:

Questions

1 maych baan jee-a dtou ree-un pee-a-saa k'mai?

   ម៉េចបានជាទៅរៀនភាសាខ្មែរ?

2 maych baan jee-a meun hao bong-aim dtay?

   ម៉េចបានជាមិនហៅបង្អែមទេ?

3 maych baan jee-a jeh pee-a-saa jeun?

   ម៉េចបានជាចេះភាសាចិន?

4 maych baan jee-a meun n'yum bai dtay?

   ម៉េចបានជាមិនញ៉ាំបាយទេ?

Answers

a bproo-ah dail t'wer gaa nou s'rok jeun.

   ព្រោះដែលធ្វើការនៅស្រុកចិន។

b bproo-ah dtou t'wer gaa nou s'rok k'mai.

   ព្រោះទៅធ្វើការនៅស្រុកខ្មែរ។

c bproo-ah meun klee-un dtay.

   ព្រោះមិនឃ្លានទេ។

d bproo-ah pa-aim bpayk.

   ព្រោះផ្អែមពេក។

Script

Consonants

There are three remaining consonant symbols, none of which occur very commonly. Here they are with their subscript forms:

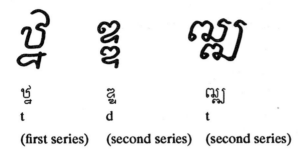

ឋ្ឋ	ឌ្ឌ	ឍ្ឍ
ឋ្ឋ	ឌ្ឌ	ឍ្ឍ
t	d	t
(first series)	(second series)	(second series)

Vowels

The final group of vowels all share the distinctive -ះ symbol which indicates that the vowel is pronounced with final aspiration.

	-ះ	-ុះ	េ-ះ	ោ-ះ
	-ះ*	-ុះ	េ-ះ	ោ-ះ
first series	-ah	-oh	-eh	-oh
second series	-ay-ah	-OOh	-ih/-eh	-oo-ah

Although the symbol also occurs in -ិះ (e.g. ជិះ **jih**), Cambodians do not include it in their normal 'lay-out' of vowel symbols in grammar books, school textbooks, etc.

*Note the very similar-looking symbol -ៈ which is pronounced **-a** after a *first series* consonant and **-ay-a** after a *second series* consonant. You will meet it later in the course in the words រយៈ ('period of time') and កុម្ភៈ ('February').

Exercise 3

Here are some of the more common words spelt with these vowels:

ផ្ដុះ   ច្រុះ   លុះ
ចេះ   នេះ   ព្រះ
កោះ   ព្រោះ   នោះ *

* Irregular pronunciation: **nOOh** and not 'noo-ah'.

How are you progressing?

You have now covered the broad basics of the Cambodian system of writing and should now be in a position to make a reasonably successful attempt at reading most Cambodian words. Inevitably there are some words which do not obey the 'rules' you have learned and whose pronunciation is not reflected by the spelling; such words simply have to be memorised.

There are still a few symbols and diacritics which you have not yet met. The most important of these are given below in the 'Miscellaneous' section. The Cambodian alphabet is also set out for you in alphabetical order in a form which you might find useful to photocopy for reference when reading the passages in the second part of this book.

Miscellaneous diacritics and symbols

Independent vowels

The remaining independent vowels are as follows:

ឫ	ឬ	ឩ	ឧ	ឱ	ឰ
-ay	-ai	-o	-oa	-ao	-ao

ឬ	ឬ	ឭ	ឮ
reu	reu	leu	leu

Some common words containing these vowels are:

ខុសភា	**OO-sa-pee-a**	May
ឱ្យ	**ao-ee**	to give, cause
ឫ	**reu**	or
ឮ	**leu**	to hear

៎

This symbol converts the *first series* consonants ប, ស, ហ, អ into *second series* consonants:

ហ៊ាន   **hee-un**   ('to dare')

Instead of writing ៎ with a superscript vowel such as ៊ី, the symbol ៊ is used:

ស៊ី   **see**

៉

Although this represents a short **a** sound, it appears most commonly in conjunction with the consonant យ to produce an **ai** sound

វិទ្យាល័យ   **weut-ta-ya-lai**   ('college')

៊

This symbol indicates that the letter beneath it should not be pronounced. It occurs in words of foreign origin and enables the foreign etymology to be preserved in the spelling:

ប្រសាសន៍   **bpra-saah**   ('word')

៌

This symbol can influence the pronunciation of a word in a number of different ways. In some words, it cancels out the letter beneath it, in others it indicates the insertion of a **ra** syllable, and in another group of words it changes the pronunciation of the inherent vowel from **-or** to **-or-a**. One of the most common words using this symbol is

ពណ៌   **bpoa-a**   ('colour')

This symbol, which looks like a tiny number eight, appears only in the words ក gor ('so', 'therefore') and ដ dor (word sometimes used to link nouns and adjectives).

Alphabet chart

The chart on pages 101 and 102 consists of a list of consonants (with their subscript forms) and vowels (excluding independent vowels) as they appear in Cambodian school primers. You may find it useful to copy the list as it appears and to shade the *second series* consonants with a luminous marker as an aid to memorising them. It will certainly be helpful to have such a sheet handy for the readings in the second half of the book, although by the end of the course you should find you need to consult it less and less frequently.

Alphabet chart

Consonants with sub-script forms

កក្	ខ្ខ	ក្ក	ឃ្ឃ	ង្ង
g	k	g	k	ng
ច្ច	ឆ្ឆ	ជ្ជ	ឈ្ឈ	ញ
j	ch	j	ch	ñ/ny
ដ្ដ	ឋ្ឋ	ឌ្ឌ	ឍ្ឍ	ណ្ណ
d	t	d	t	n
ត្ត	ថ្ថ	ទ្ទ	ធ្ធ	ន្ន
dt	t	dt	t	n
ប្ប	ផ្ផ	ព្ព	ភ្ភ	ម្ម
b	p	bp	p	m
យ្យ	រ្រ	ល្ល	វ្វ	ស្ស
y	r	l	w	s
ហ្ហ	ឡ្ឡ	អ្អ		
h	l	zero		

Vowels

	-or	-aa	-e	-ay	-eu	-eu
1st series	-or	-aa	-e	-ay	-eu	-eu
2nd series	-or	-ee-a	-i	-ee	-eu	-eu

	-o	-oa	-oo-a
	-u	-oo	-oo-a

	-ar	-eu-a	-ee-a	-ay
	-er	-eu-a	-ee-a	-ay

	-ai	-ai	-ao	-ao
	-air	-ay-ee	-oa	-ou

	-om	-om	-um	-ah
	-OOm	-OOm	-oa-um	-ay-ah

	-oh	-eh	-oh
	-ooh	-ih	-oo-ah

10 ree-un saa jee-a t'may

Review

This unit reviews the ground covered in Lessons 6–9. Again, if you find you are struggling, go back over these units before attempting to proceed with the course.

Exercise 1 📼

How would you say the following in Cambodian? (Feel free to 'cheat' by reading the Cambodian script prompts!)

1 Do you know the Olympic Stadium?

ស្គាល់អូឡាំពិកស្ថាល់ទេ?

2 How much to go to O Russei Market?

ទៅផ្សារ អូរុស្សី ថ្លៃប៉ុន្មាន?

3 It's not very far. មិនឆ្ងាយប៉ុន្មានទេ ។

Normally I go for 50 riels. ធម្មតាខ្ញុំទៅតែហាសិប

រៀលទេ ។

4 Turn left and then go straight on.

បត់ទៅខាងឆ្វេងហើយទៅមុខត្រង់។

5 Please take me to Wat Phnom. សូមជូនខ្ញុំទៅវត្តភ្នំ។

6 Please bring me the menu. សូមយកតារាងម្ហូបមកមើល។

7 I can't eat hot (spicy) food. ខ្ញុំញ៉ាំម្ហូបហឹរមិនបានទេ ។

8 I'd like a bottle of Coca Cola ខ្ញុំចង់បានកូកា-

and a plate of chicken fried rice. កូឡាម្ខយដបហើយ

នឹងព្យាយនាសាច់មាន់មួយចាន។

9 Does it taste good?

ឆ្ងាញ់ទេ?

10 It doesn't taste good. It's too sweet.

មិនឆ្ងាញ់ទេ ផ្អែមពេក។

11 I can't eat it. I'm full.

ខ្ញុំញ៉ាំមិនបានទេ ។ ឆ្អែតហើយ ។

12 I'm not very hungry.

ខ្ញុំមិនឃ្លានទេ។

13 Excuse me please, where's the toilet?

សូមទោស បង្គន់នៅឯណា?

14 Could I have the bill please?

សូមគិតលុយ?

15 Hello. How are you?

សួស្តី សុខសប្បាយជាទេ?

16 I'm delighted to meet you.

ខ្ញុំត្រេកអរដែលបាន ស្គាល់លោក។

17 How come you speak Cambodian?

ម៉េចបានជាលោកចេះខ្មែរ?

18 I used to work in a camp
   (ជំរំ) in Thailand.

ខ្ញុំដែលធ្វើការនៅជំរំ នៅស្រុកថៃ ។

19 At that time I had lots of
   Cambodian friends.

ពេលនោះខ្ញុំមានពួកម៉ាក ខ្មែរច្រើន។

Exercise 2

Read the following Cambodian words:

ច្រើន	ប្រាប់	ដែល	ទឹក	ម្ហូប
ចុះ	ដេក	ព្រោះ	ខ្ញុំ	ស្គា
នាក់	ម្ចាយ	ស្ងាត	ដប់	ប៉ុ
ផ្ទះ	ខ្ទិពុក	ឯណា	គេ	ប៉ុន្មាន
មែន	ឆ្ងាញ់	ចេះ	ឬ	ស៊ី
ថ្ងៃ	សាច់	ភ្នំ	ឥឡូវ	ឈប់

11 dtoo-ra-sup

A telephone call

In this lesson you will learn about:

- the language of telephone calls
- *when?* questions
- telling the time

Cambodian has two words for 'telephone' – **dtoo-ra-sup** which is borrowed from Thai, and **dtay-lay-foan** which comes from French. Both words can be used as either nouns or verbs. In the dialogue that follows, Paul seems to find making a phone call in a foreign language rather less stressful than most beginners. If you are planning to make a call in Cambodian, it might be a good idea to have the 'More useful expressions' list close at hand, too!

dtoo-ra-sup ▭▭

A: Paul; B: Mr Som Sok's wife; C: Mr Som Sok

A: aa-loa aa-loa អាឡូ អាឡូ

   k'nyom soam ni-yee-ay neung ខ្ញុំសូមនិយាយនឹង

   loak Sorm Sok baan dtay? លោក សម សុខ បានទេ?

B: jaa soam jum moo-ay plairt ចាំ សូមចាំមួយភ្លែត

   k'nyom dtou jOOm-ree-up goa-ut. ខ្ញុំទៅជំរាបគាត់។

C: soo-a s'day k'nyom Sok. សួរស្ដី ខ្ញុំសុខ។

   nay-uk naa neung? អ្នកណាហ្នឹង?

A: soo-a s'day loak Sok   សួរស្ដីលោកសុខ
    k'nyom Paul.   ខ្ញុំ Paul។

C: loak Paul reu dtay?   លោក Paul ឬទេ?
    moak s'rok k'mai bpee ong-gul?   មកស្រុកខ្មែរពីអង្កាល់?

A: bpee m'seul meuñ.   ពីម្សិលមិញ។
    ay-lou nih som-nuk nou   ឥឡូវនេះសំណាក់នៅ
    son-ta-gee ma-noa-rom.   សណ្ឋាគារមនោរម្យ។

C: meun deung taa t'ngai nih Paul   មិនដឹងថា ថ្ងៃនេះ Paul
    dtOOm-nay reu dtay?   ទំនេរ ឬទេ?

A: t'ngai nih meun sou   ថ្ងៃនេះមិនសូវ
    dtOOm-nay dtay.   ទំនេរ ទេ។
    sa-aik nou bpayl l'ngee-ich   ស្អែក នៅពេលល្ងាច
    s'roo-ul jee-ung.   ស្រួលជាង។

B: bar uñ-jeung k'nyom neung moak   បើអញ្ជឹង ខ្ញុំនឹងមក
    joo-up nou maong bprum gon-lah   ជួបនៅម៉ោងប្រាំកន្លះ
    hai-ee yerng neung dtou n'yum   ហើយយើងនឹងទៅញ៉ាំ
    bai jee-a-moo-ay k'nee-a.   បាយជាមួយគ្នា ។

A: *Hello, Hello.*
    Can I speak to Mr Som Sok, please?
B: *Yes, please wait a moment.*
C: *Hello, Sok speaking. Who's that?*
A: *Hello Sok. This is Paul.*
C: *Paul? When did you arrive in Cambodia?*
A: *Yesterday. At the moment I'm staying at the Manorom Hotel.*
C: *I don't know whether you're free today?*
A: *I'm not really free today. Tomorrow, early evening would be better.*
C: *In that case I'll come and meet you at half-past five and we'll go and have a meal together.*

Vocabulary

soam ni-yee-ay neung	could I speak to . . .	សូមនិយាយនឹង . . .
jum	to wait	ចាំ
soam jum . . .	please wait	សូមចាំ
moo-ay plairt	a moment	មួយភ្លែត . . .
neung	this, there	ហ្នឹង
neung	will (future tense)	នឹង
bpayl l'ngee-ich	evening	ពេលល្ងាច

More useful expressions

I can't hear you.
k'nyom s'dup meun leu dtay. ខ្ញុំស្ដាប់មិនឮទេ។

Does anyone speak English?
mee-un nay-uk naa jeh ong-klayh dtay?

មានអ្នកណាចេះអង់គ្លេសទេ?

Please say that again.
soam taa m'dorng dtee-ut. សូមថាម្ដងទៀត។

Please speak slowly.
soam ni-yee-ay moo-ay moo-ay. សូមនិយាយមួយ ១។

Please speak loudly.
soam ni-yee-ay klung klung. សូមនិយាយខ្លាំង ១។

Please call back in an hour.
moo-ay maong dtee-ut soam មួយម៉ោងទៀត

dtay-lay-foan m'dorng dtee-ut. សូមតេឡេហ្វូនម្ដងទៀត។

I'll call back tomorrow.
sa-aik k'nyom neung dtay-lay-foan ស្អែកខ្ញុំនឹងតេឡេហ្វូន

m'dorng dtee-ut. ម្ដងទៀត។

Language points

When?

If a question refers to the past then the word for 'when?' is **bpee ong-gul**. If the question refers to the future, **ong-gul** is used on its own:

ror-dtayh plerng jeuñ *ong-gul?* របទេះភ្លើងចេញអង្កាល់?
When does the train leave?

yerng joo-up k'nee-a *ong-gul?* យើងជួបគ្នាអង្កាល់?
When shall we meet?

loak moak dol bpee *ong-gul?* លោកមកដល់ពីអង្កាល់?
When did you arrive?

goa-ut dtou bpee *ong-gul?* គាត់ទៅពីអង្កាល់?
When did he go?

Units of time

Here are the basic units of time. The days of the week and months appear in Lesson 14.

day	**t'ngai**	ថ្ងៃ
today	**t'ngai nih**	ថ្ងៃនេះ
yesterday	**m'seul meuñ**	ម្សិលមិញ
tomorrow	**sa-aik**	ស្អែក
week	**aa-dteut**	អាទិត្យ
this week	**aa-dteut nih**	អាទិត្យនេះ
last week	**aa-dteut mOOn**	អាទិត្យមុន
next week	**aa-dteut grao-ee**	អាទិត្យក្រោយ
month	**kai**	ខែ
year	**ch'num**	ឆ្នាំ
morning	**bpreuk**	ព្រឹក
noon	**t'ngai dtrong**	ថ្ងៃត្រង់
(early) afternoon	**ra-see-ul**	រសៀល

(late) afternoon/ early evening	lngee-ich	ល្ងាច
night	yOOp	យប់
last night	yOOp meuñ	យប់មិញ
day time	bpayl t'ngai	ពេលថ្ងៃ
night time	bpayl yOOp	ពេលយប់
hour	maong	ម៉ោង
minute	nee-a-dtee	នាទី
second	wi-nee-a-dtee	វិនាទី

Future tense

When the word **neung** occurs in front of the main verb, it indicates a future tense. Often, however, **neung** is omitted and the context of the sentence is sufficient to make it clear that the future is being referred to:

yerng (*neung*) dtou sa-aik. យើង(នឹង)ទៅស្អែក។
We *shall* go tomorrow.

goa-ut (*neung*) ree-un   គាត់ (នឹង) រៀនភាសាខ្មែរ។
pee-a-sah k'mai.
He *will* learn Cambodian.

Telling the time

The hour times are expressed by the pattern **maong** ('hour') + number. The word **hai-ee** ('already') is added after the number word to mean 'It's . . . o'clock':

maong boo-un (hai-ee).   ម៉ោងបួន (ហើយ)។
It's four o'clock.

maong bprum-bpeul (hai-ee). ម៉ោងប្រាំពីរ (ហើយ)។
It's seven o'clock.

Minutes past the hour are expressed by the pattern **maong** + number of hour + **neung** ('and') + number of minutes + **nee-a-dtee** ('minute'):

maong bprum neung dop nee-a-dtee   ម៉ោងប្រាំនឹងដប់នាទី
ten past five

Minutes to the hour are expressed by the pattern **maong** + number of hour + **kwah** ('lack') + number of minutes + **nee-a-dtee**:

> **maong bprum-moo-ay kwah dop** ម៉ោងប្រាំមួយខ្វះដប់នាទី
> **nee-a-dtee**
> ten to six

Half-hours are expressed using the word **gon-lah**:

> **maong bprum-boo-un** *gon-lah* ម៉ោងប្រាំបួនកន្លះ
> *half past* nine

There is no special word for quarter hours; they are expressed as fifteen minutes past or to the hour.

The question word **bpon-maan** is used to ask questions about the time:

> **maong** *bpon-maan* **(hai-ee)?** ម៉ោងប៉ុន្មានហើយ?
> *What* time is it?

> **goa-ut moak (nou) maong** គាត់មក(នៅ)ម៉ោងប៉ុន្មាន?
> *bpon-maan?*
> *What* time is he coming?

Pronunciation practice 〔CO〕

This exercise focuses on a number of initial consonant clusters which do not occur in English. If you have the tape, you will hear each word spoken twice. Listen, then repeat the words after the speaker.

ឈ្មោះ	ឆ្ងាយ	ឆ្នាំ	ឆ្វេង	ច្រើន	ប្ដី
'name'	'far'	'year'	'left'	'many'	'husband'

ម្ហូប	ស្ដាំ	ស្រី	ថ្លៃ	ថ្ងៃ	ធ្វើ
'food'	'right'	'woman'	'price'	'day'	'do, make'

Exercise 1 〔CO〕

You need to make phone calls to these Cambodian friends. How would you ask to speak to them?

1 លោក គាន់ យុន

2 អ្នកស្រី មាស សុជាតិ

3 លោក ពៅ ទីតា
4 អ្នកស្រី គិមម៉ុ

Exercise 2 📼

maong bpon-maan hai-ee?   ម៉ោងប៉ុន្មានហើយ?

1 ១១.៤៥

2 ១៧.៣០

3 ០៦.២៥

4 ១០.០០

5 ១៦.១៥

Exercise 3

How would you say:

1 When did you arrive in England?
2 What time do you go to work?
3 When will you go to Cambodia?
4 What time is it?
5 When shall we meet?

Cambodian voices (1) 📼

**bpayl t'ngai t'wer gaa nou gaa-ri-yaa-lai
. . . bpayl yOOp t'wer gaa nou poa-ja-nee-
ya-taan**
*In the daytime I work in an office . . . in the
evening I work in a restaurant*

On the tape you will hear a young Cambodian typist talking about her working hours. What time does she start work at her office and what time does she finish? What does she do in the evening? Why?

You may find it helpful to have the vocabulary list in front of you as you listen, and you will certainly need to listen to the passage a number of times. When you have got as much out of the passage as

you can from listening, study the Cambodian transcript of the tape, below.

Vocabulary

អ្នករាយអង្គុលីលេខ	typist	ប៉ុណ្ណោះ	only
ការិយាល័យ	office	ហេតុ	reason
ចូល	to enter	ឆ្លៀតពេល	to take the
ចេញ	to leave		opportunity
ពី … ទៅ	from … to	រហូត	throughout
សំរាក	to rest, relax	ដល់	until; to arrive at,
ប្រាក់	money		reach
ប្រាក់ខែ	salary	ពាក់កណ្ដាល	middle
គ្រប់គ្រាន់	enough	អធ្រាត	night, midnight
ចិញ្ចឹម	to support	ទើប	then
ល្មម	enough	មក … វិញ	to return
ចាយ	to pay for	ផ្ទះ	house, home

ខ្ញុំឈ្មោះ សុខា ធ្វើការ ជាអ្នករាយអង្គុលីលេខនៅការិយាល័យ នៅក្រុងភ្នំពេញ។ ខ្ញុំធ្វើការមួយថ្ងៃប្រាំបីម៉ោង។ ខ្ញុំចូល ធ្វើការនៅពេលព្រឹក ម៉ោងប្រាំពីរកន្លះ ចេញធ្វើការ នៅពេលល្ងាចម៉ោងប្រាំកន្លះ។ នៅថ្ងៃត្រង់ ពីម៉ោង ដប់ពីរទៅម៉ោងពីររសៀល ជាពេលសំរាក។

ប្រាក់ខែរបស់ខ្ញុំ មិនគ្រប់គ្រាន់ចិញ្ចឹមគ្រួសារទេ
ល្មមតែខ្ញុំម្នាក់ឯងចាយប៉ុណ្ណោះ ។ ហេតុនេះខ្ញុំ
ត្រូវឆ្លៀតពេលយប់ទៅធ្វើការនៅភោជនីយដ្ឋាន
ទៀត របហូតដល់ពាក់កណ្ដាលអធ្រាតទើបមកដល់
ផ្ទះវិញ ។

Questions

The questions that follow are straightforward comprehension
questions based on the passage you have just listened to and/or
read. By writing a full sentence answer you will help to reinforce
your command of Cambodian grammar as well as improving your
handwriting and spelling!

១ សុខាធ្វើការអ្វី?

២ ធ្វើការនៅឯណា?

៣. ធ្វើការមួយថ្ងៃប៉ុន្មានម៉ោង ?

៤ ចូលធ្វើការម៉ោងប៉ុន្មាន?

៥ ចេញធ្វើការម៉ោងប៉ុន្មាន?

៦ នៅថ្ងៃត្រង់សំរាកប៉ុន្មានម៉ោង?

៧ ប្រាក់ខែរបស់សុខា គ្រប់គ្រាន់ចិញ្ចឹមគ្រួសារឬទេ?

៨ ហេតុអ្វីបានជាសុខាត្រូវទៅធ្វើការពេលយប់?

៩ ធ្វើការនៅឯណា?

12 nou dtee p'saa

At the market

In this lesson you will learn about:

- asking what things are called
- **ch'nguñ meun ch'nguñ**
- **bpoo-uk**

In this and subsequent units an additional reading passage is included which is aimed to both expand your vocabulary and develop your 'reading stamina'. It is probably best to practise reading the new words in isolation first, in the vocabulary lists. There is no magic way to ensure that you will be able to remember them, but copying them a number of times, or, better still, copying down the phrase in which they occur in the text, is for most people a reasonably effective strategy.

Do not be surprised if at this stage in the book you find that your progress appears to slow down. The aim now is to try to wean you from dependency on romanised Cambodian and to expose you to a much wider range of vocabulary and sentence structure. Be prepared to take your time. Work slowly through the passages. Read each one at least half a dozen times. This will improve your reading speed, your vocabulary retention and your subconscious absorption of Cambodian grammar.

nou dtee p'saa ⬚

Generally speaking, markets are excellent places to practise your Cambodian, and often, for the cost of a very small purchase, you can get a valuable language lesson from vendors. This lesson gives you practice in two basic transactions – bargaining and asking names of things. See how much of the dialogue you can read in Cambodian script now!

> A: Jill; B: vendor

A:	soam soo-a nih hao taa ay?	សូមសួរ នេះហៅថាអ្វី?
B:	hao taa groa-ich.	ហៅថា ក្រូច។
A:	moo-ay gee-loa bpon-maan ree-ul?	មួយគីឡូរ ប៉ុន្នាន រៀល?
B:	bay roy ree-ul.	បីរយរៀល។
A:	bay roy ree-ul?	បីរយរៀល?
	oa t'lai nah.	អ៊ូ ថ្លៃណាស់។
	joh t'lai bpon-dteuch baan dtay?	ចុះ ថ្លៃបន្តិចបានទេ?
B:	dtay meun t'lai dtay.	ទេ មិនថ្លៃទេ។
	groa-ich nih ch'nguñ nah.	ក្រូចនេះ ឆ្ងាញ់ណាស់
	lor merl ch'nguñ meun ch'nguñ?	លមើល ឆ្ងាញ់មិនឆ្ងាញ់?
A:	ch'nguñ kroa-un bar.	ឆ្ងាញ់ គ្រាន់បើ។
	bpee roy ree-ul baan dtay?	ពីររយរៀលបានទេ?
A:	meun baan dtay.	មិនបានទេ។
	jong baan bpon-maan gee-loa?	ចង់ បានប៉ុន្មានគីឡូ?

B: k'nyom jong baan dtai moo-ay   ខ្ញុំចង់បានតែមួយ
      gee-loa dtay.   គីឡូវទេ។

A: *Could I ask what these are called?*
B: *They're called 'oranges'.*
A: *How much a kilo are they?*
B: *Three hundred riels.*
A: *Three hundred riels? That's expensive.*
B: *No. It's not.*
   These oranges are very tasty.
   Try them. Aren't they tasty?
A: *Yes, they are.*
   How about 200 riels?
B: *No, I can't.*
   How many kilos do you want?
A: *I only want one kilo.*

Vocabulary

groa-ich	orange(s)	ក្រូច
lor merl	to try out	លមើល
ch'nguñ meun ch'nguñ	is it tasty?	ឆ្ងាញ់មិនឆ្ងាញ់?
kroa-un bar	quite well; enough	គ្រាន់បើ
soam	I'd like (to)	សូម
soo-a	to ask	សូមសួរ
hao	to call; be called	ហៅ
hao taa	it's called	ហៅថា
joh t'lai	to lower the price	ចុះថ្លៃ
bar	if	បើ

Language points

Finding out names of things

nih hao taa ay?   នេះហៅថាអ្វី?
What's this called?

pee-a-saa k'mai (hao) taa ay?　ភាសាខ្មែរ(ហៅ)ថាអ្វី ?
What do you say in Cambodian?

s'ay nih (*colloquial*)　ស្អីនេះ?
What's this?

nih a-way　នេះ អ្វី?
What's this?

ch'nguñ meun ch'nguñ?

This pattern ('tasty not tasty?') is common in spoken Cambodian:

dtou meun dtou?　ទៅមិនទៅ?
Are you going or not?

t'lai meun t'lai?　ថ្លៃមិនថ្លៃ?
Is it expensive or not?

bpoo-uk

The word **bpoo-uk** ('group') is sometimes used in front of a noun to indicate a plural meaning:

dol bpoo-uk dtee-a-hee-un yoo-un joal moak ...
ដល់ពួកទាហានយួនចូលមក ...
When the Vietnamese soldiers came in ...

Its usage often corresponds to the English use of the plural when making generalisations:

bpoo-uk baa-rung n'yum m'hoap heul meun baan dtay.
ពួកបារាំងញ៉ាំម្ហូបហឹរមិនបានទេ ។
Westerners can't eat spicy food.

Pronunciation practice　[CO]

This exercise gives you a chance to practise words ending in final **p**, **t** or **k** sounds. Be careful not to 'release' the final consonant in the way that you would when pronouncing English words.

ទឹក	លោក	ឪពុក	ពេក
'water'	'you'	'father'	'too'

ឈប់	ម្ហូប	ស្ដាប់	ដប
'stop'	'food'	'listen'	'bottle'
ព្រាទ	បត់	កើត	ស្អាត
'yes'	'turn'	'be born'	'clean; beautiful'

Cambodian voices (2) 📼

**bpoo-uk 'nay-uk t'may' meun t'loa-up
neung t'wer gaa haal t'ngai haal plee-ung**
*The 'new people' weren't used to working
out in the open exposed to the elements*

The speaker on your tape is an elderly farmer who talks about life
in his village during the Lon Nol government (1970–5) and the Pol

Pot period (1975–8).

Vocabulary

ចំការ	farm, market garden	ប្រជាជន	people
		ចាស់	old
		ធ្លាប់នឹង	used to, accustomed to
រស់នៅ	to live		
ភូមិ	village	ហាល	to expose to
តាំងពី	since	ថ្ងៃ	sun; day
កើត	to be born	ភ្លៀង	rain
ម្ល៉េះ	so, such	ហាលថ្ងៃហាលភ្លៀង	
លន់ នល់	Lon Nol		exposed to the elements
ចេះតែ …	to be always … -ing		
		ដូច	like, as
ទម្លាក់	to drop	ជម្ងឺ	disease
គ្រាប់បែក	bomb	រហូតដល់	all the way to
លើ	on	ជីវិត	life
វាល(ស្រែ)	field (rice)	បង់ជីវិត	to lose one's life
សម្លាប់	to kill	ថ្នំពេទ្យ	medicine
មនុស្ស	person	ខ្វះខាត	to lack
មិនតិចទេ	not a little	ទាហាន	soldier
ជាច្រើន	a lot	យួន	Vietnamese
ពួក	group; *plural marker*	ទើប	then
		ចាក	to depart, leave
ឲ្យ	to give	ត្រឡប់ទៅ	to return
ថ្មី	new	… វិញ	
'អ្នកថ្មី'	'new people'		
ឬ	or		

ខ្ញុំឈ្មោះ កុយ អាយុហុកសិបបីឆ្នាំ។ ខ្ញុំរស់នៅ

ក្នុងភូមិនេះតាំងពីខ្ញុំកើតមកម្ល៉េះ។ នៅពេល
លន់ នល់ ធ្វើស្រេចការពិប្ហាកណាស់ អាមេរិកាំង
ចេះតែមកទម្លាក់គ្រាប់បែកលើវាលស្រែ សម្លាប់
មនុស្សមិនតិចទេ។ ដល់ពេលប៉ុល ពត មានអ្នក
ភ្ញៀវពេញជាច្រើនមកនៅក្នុងភូមិខ្ញុំ។ ពួកអ្នកក្រុង
ទាំងនោះ គេឲ្យឈ្មោះ ថា 'អ្នកថ្មី' ឬ 'ប្រជាជនថ្មី'
ៗពួកខ្ញុំ គេឲ្យឈ្មោះ ថា 'អ្នកចាស់' ឬ 'ប្រជាជនចាស់'
ពួកអ្នកថ្មីដែលមករស់នៅក្នុងភូមិខ្ញុំជាច្រើន មិនធ្លាប់នឹង
ធ្វើការហាលថ្ងៃហាលភ្លៀងដូចពួកខ្ញុំទេ មិនយូរប៉ុន្មាន
ក៏ទៅជាមានជម្ងឺរហូតដល់ស្លាប់បង់ជីវិតទៅ ព្រោះពេល
នោះ ពេទ្យក៏គ្មាន ថ្នាំពេទ្យក៏ខ្វះខាត។
ដល់ពួកទាហានយួនចូលមក អ្នកក្រុងទាំងនោះទើបចាក
ចេញពីភូមិខ្ញុំ ត្រឡប់ទៅក្រុងភ្នំពេញវិញទៅ។

Questions

1 What problems did farmers in Goy's village face during the Lon Nol period?

2 Who were អ្នកថ្មី and អ្នកចាស់?

3 During the Pol Pot period, what was the major cause of death in Goy's village?

When you have worked out the answers to these questions you might like to try those below!

១ ម៉េចបានជាធ្វើស្រែចការ ពេលលន់ នល់ ពិប្ហាកណាស់?

២ ពេលប៉ុល ពត មាន អ្នកណាមកនៅក្នុងភូមិកុយ?

៣ ពេលប៉ុល ពត គេឲ្យពួកអ្នកក្រុងឈ្មោះ ថាអ្វី?

៤ អ្នកធ្វើស្រែដែលរស់នៅក្នុងភូមិតាំងពីកើត
គេឲ្យឈ្មោះ ថាអ្វី?

...gual Cambodian is also available in the form of a course pack (ISBN 0-415-10008-9), containing this book and two cassettes. The cassettes include pronunciation practice, dialogues and role-playing exercises, recorded by native speakers of Cambodian, and are an invaluable aid to improving your language skills.

If you have been unable to obtain the course pack, the double cassette (ISBN 0-415-10007-0) can be ordered separately through your bookseller or, in case of difficulty, send payment with order to Routledge Ltd, ITPS, Cheriton House, North Way, Andover, Hants SP10 5BE, or to Routledge Inc., 29 West 35th Street, New York, NY 10001, USA.

The publishers reserve the right to change prices without notice.

CASSETTES ORDER FORM

Please supply one/two/ .... double cassette(s) of

Colloquial Cambodian, Smyth.
ISBN 0-415-10007-0

Price   £15.99* incl. VAT
         $22.95*

☐ I enclose payment with order.
☐ Please debit my Access/Mastercharge/Mastercard/Visa/American Express. Account number:

Expiry date ....

Name ....

Address ....

....

Date ....

Signature ....

Order from your bookseller or from:

ROUTLEDGE LTD
ITPS
Cheriton House
North Way
Andover
Hants
SP10 5BE
ENGLAND

ROUTLEDGE INC.
29 West 35th Street
New York
NY 10001
USA

៥ ពួកអ្នកថ្មីធ្លាប់នឹងធ្វើការហាលថ្ងៃហាលភ្លៀងឬទេ?

៦ ម៉េចបានជាអ្នកថ្មីនៅភូមិកុយស្លាប់ពេលប៉ុល ពត?

៧ ដល់ពួកទាហានយួនចូលមក អ្នកក្រុងធ្វើអ្វី?

ផ្សារ 🔳

This passage introduces you to the names of the major markets in Phnom Penh and the goods that are sold in them.

Vocabulary

ត្រប់	every	របស់	things
ស្រុក	district	ផ្លែឈើ	fruit
យុំ	town	បន្លែ	vegetable
នៃ	of	សំលៀកបំពាក់	clothes
តែង ... (+verb)	always ...	សៀវភៅ	books
សំរាប់	for	គ្រឿង	utensil, tool
អ្នករកស៊ី	businessman	ប្រើ	to use
លក់	to sell	ក្នុង	in
ដូរ	to exchange	ទិញ	to buy
ទំនិញ	merchandise, goods	អ្វីមួយ	any
		តថ្លៃ	to bargain the price
ផ្សេង ៗ	various	ប្រគល់	to give, hand over
មានឈ្មោះល្បី	to be famous		
ក្រៅពី	besides	ប្រាក់	money
ជាដើម	for example	ដូរ ... វិញ	to change back

នៅគ្រប់ខេត្ត ស្រុក យុំ ភូមិនៃប្រទេសកម្ពុជាតែងមាន ផ្សារធំតូចសំរាប់អ្នករកស៊ីលក់ដូរទំនិញផ្សេង ៗ ។

នៅក្រុងភ្នំពេញ ផ្សារដែលមានឈ្មោះល្បីជាងគេ
គឺផ្សារថ្មី ឬផ្សារធំ។ ក្រៅពីនេះមានផ្សារកណ្ដាល
ផ្សារចាស់ ផ្សារ អូឡាំពិក និងផ្សារ អូឬស្សីជាដើម។

នៅផ្សារទាំងនោះ គេលក់របស់ផ្សេង ៗ មានផ្លែឈើ
បន្លែ ត្រី សាច់ សំលៀកបំពាក់ សៀវភៅ ហើយនិង
គ្រឿងសំរាប់ប្រើក្នុងផ្ទះ។

មុននឹងទិញរបស់អ្វីមួយ យើងអាចតថ្លៃបានតែបើ
ប្រគល់ប្រាក់ហើយ ៗ ចង់ដូររបស់ជាប្រាក់វិញ
និងមានពិបាកច្រើន។

13 doa loo-ee neung dteuñ dtaim

Changing money and buying stamps

> **In this lesson you will learn about:**
>
> - using **baan** in expressions of time
> - passive constructions
> - *not . . . at all*

The Cambodian unit of currency is the *riel*. There are no coins and the most commonly circulating banknotes are those with denominations of 50, 100, 200 and 500 riels. Rampant inflation during the early 1990s made it a particularly unstable currency and many people prefer to conduct business in US dollars and in some cases, Thai *baht*. In Phnom Penh, money can be changed in banks (**tor-nee-a-gee-a**) or with the numerous money changers along the main streets and near the markets.

doa loo-ee neung dteuñ dtaim 🔲

> A: Frank; B: bank employee

A:	k'nyom jong doa loo-ee klah.	ខ្ញុំចង់ដូរលុយខ្លះ។
	jong doa dol-laa aa-may-ri-gung	ចង់ដូរដុល្លារអាមេរិកាំង
	jee-a loo-ee ree-ul.	ជាលុយរៀល។
B:	baat doa bpon-maan dol-laa?	ប្រាទ ដូរ ប៉ុន្មានដុល្លា?
A:	t'ngai nih moo-ay dol-laa	ថ្ងៃនេះមួយដុល្លា
	bpon-maan ree-ul?	ប៉ុន្មានរៀល?

| B: | moo-ay dol-laa doa bprum roy ree-ul. | មួយដុល្លាដូរ ប្រាំរយ រៀល។ |
| A: | k'nyom jong doa haa seup dol-laa. | ខ្ញុំចង់ដូរ ហាសិបដុល្លា។ |

A: *I want to change some money.*
I want to change US dollars into riels.
B: *Yes. How many dollars are you changing?*
A: *Today how many riels are there to the dollar?*
B: *Five hundred riels to the dollar.*
A: *I want to change 50 dollars.*

Vocabulary

tor-nee-a-gee-a	bank	ធនាគារ
doa	to change	ដូរ
loo-ee	money	លុយ

klah	some	ខ្លះ
dol-laa	dollar	ដុល្លា

A: Frank; B: Post Office clerk

A:	k'nyom jong p'nyar som-bot nih dtou s'rok ong-klayh.	ខ្ញុំចង់ផ្ញើសំបុត្រនេះ ទៅស្រុកអង់គ្លេស។
B:	p'nyar dtou dtaam ga-bul hoh reu ga-bul dteuk?	ផ្ញើទៅតាមកប៉ាល់ហោះ ឬកប៉ាល់ទឹក?
A:	dtaam ga-bul hoh.	តាមកប៉ាល់ហោះ។
B:	m'roy ree-ul.	មួយរយរៀល។
A:	hai-ee k'nyom soam dtaim haa seup	ហើយខ្ញុំសូមតែមប្រាំ ហាសិប
	ree-ul boo-un son-leuk porng.	រៀល បួនសន្លឹកផង។
B:	t'lai dtay-ung oh bay roy ree-ul.	ថ្លៃទាំងអស់បីរយរៀល ។

A: *I want to send this letter to England.*
B: *Are you sending it by air or sea?*
A: *By air.*
B: *One hundred riels.*
A: *And I want four 50-riel stamps, too.*
B: *Altogether that's three hundred riels.*

Vocabulary

bprai-sa-nee-ya-taan	post office	ប្រៃសណីយដ្ឋាន
p'nyar	send	ផ្ញើ
som-bot	letter	សំបុត្រ
dtaam	by; according to	តាម
ga-bul hoh	aeroplane	កប៉ាល់ហោះ
dtaam ga-bul hoh	by air	តាមកប៉ាល់ហោះ
ga-bul dteuk	ship	កប៉ាល់ទឹក

dtaim	stamp	តែមប្រិ៍
son-leuk	classifier for stamps	សន្លឹក

Pronunciation practice 🔲

In this lesson there is further practice on final consonant sounds, this time emphasising words ending in -ញ and -ច. The final -ច is a problem for many people learning Cambodian.

ឆ្ងាញ់	ទិញ	ចេញ	ដេញ	ភ្នំពេញ
'tasty'	'buy'	'depart'	'chase out'	'Phnom Penh'
សាច់	មិនបាច់	រួច	ខូច	សើច
'meat'	'not necessary'	'then'	'broken'	'laugh'
បន្តិចបន្តួច	ក្រូច	ដូច	តូច	ម៉េច
'a little'	'orange(s)'	'like, as'	'small'	'how, why'

Cambodian voices (3) 🔲

t'wer s'rai nou poom k'nyom bpi-baak nah
Farming in my village is very difficult

On the tape you will hear a Phnom Penh cyclo driver explaining why he left his home province to come and work in Phnom Penh. Without reading the transcript, see how quickly you can find out (*a*) what province he came from, (*b*) how long he has been working in Phnom Penh and (*c*) what he used to do in his home village. You will need to study the new vocabulary before you will understand his reasons for leaving home.

Vocabulary

រកស៊ី	to earn a living	តាប់បែកកប់	mine
អ្នកធាក់ស៊ីក្លូ	cyclo driver	ស្ទើរតែ	almost
កាលពីមុននេះ	formerly	កន្លែង	place
គ្រោះថ្នាក់	danger	ត្រូវ	*passive marker*

របួស	to be wounded, injured	អ្នកភូមិ	villager
ដោយ	by	ហ៊ាន	to dare to do something
សព្វថ្ងៃនេះ	nowadays, these days	ហេតុ	reason
		ក៏	then, so
គ្មាន ... ឡើយ	there aren't any ... at all	សំរេចចិត្ត	to decide
		នាំ	to take, bring
អ្នកណា	who?; anyone		

ខ្ញុំមកពីខេត្តស្ទឹងត្រែង។ ខ្ញុំមកនៅភ្នំពេញរកស៊ីជា
អ្នកធាក់ស៊ីក្លូបានដប់ប្រាំបីខែហើយ។ កាលពីមុននេះ
ខ្ញុំជាអ្នកធ្វើស្រែទេ ប៉ុន្តែធ្វើស្រែចការនៅស្រុកខ្ញុំឥឡូវ
ពិបាកណាស់ មានគ្រោះថ្នាក់ច្រើនព្រោះមានគ្រាប់បែកកប់
ស្ទើរតែគ្រប់កន្លែង។ នៅភូមិខ្ញុំ មានអ្នកភូមិជាច្រើន
ត្រូវស្លាប់ឬរបួសដោយគ្រាប់បែកកប់។ សព្វថ្ងៃនេះ
ស្ទើរតែគ្មានអ្នកភូមិណាហ៊ានដើរឆ្ងាយពីភូមិឡើយ។
ហេតុនេះខ្ញុំសំរេចចិត្តនាំប្រពន្ធកូនមករស់នៅក្នុង
ក្រុងភ្នំពេញទៅ។

Language points

baan *(iii)*

You have already met several uses of the word **baan**. Another usage, of which there is an example in this passage, is before expressions of past time, when it can be translated as 'for':

k'nyom ree-un k'mai *baan* bpee kai. ខ្ញុំរៀនខ្មែរ បានពីរខែ។

I have studied Cambodian *for* two months.

Passive

The passive voice is used far less frequently in Cambodian than in English. It is formed using the word **dtrou** in front of the verb. The agent can be inserted between **dtrou** and the main verb:

goa-ut dtrou dtom-roo-ut jup. គាត់ត្រូវតម្រួតចាប់។
He was arrested by the police.

'Not . . . at all'

The negative **meun** can be intensified by adding **lar-ee** at the end of the phrase:

meun la-or lar-ee មិនល្អឡើយ
not good at all

k'mee-un lar-ee. គ្មានឡើយ។
there aren't (any) at all.

Exercise 1

Fill in the missing word:

១ ខ្ញុំមកនៅភ្នំពេញរកសុីជាអ្នកធាក់សុីក្លូ ... ដប់ប្រាំបី
ខែហើយ ។
២ មានគ្រាប់បែកកប់ ... គ្រប់កន្លែង ។
៣ សព្វថ្ងៃនេះ ... គ្មានអ្នកភូមិណាហ៊ានដើរឆ្ងាយពីភូមិឡើយ។
៤ មានអ្នកភូមិជាច្រើន ... ស្លាប់ឬរបួសដោយគ្រាប់
បែកកប់ ។

Exercise 2

How would you say:

1 How much does it cost to send this letter to England?
2 I want to send this letter by air mail.
3 I would like three 100-riel stamps and two 50-riel stamps.
4 How many riels to the dollar?
5 I want to change 100 dollars into riels.

អំពីប្រជាជាតិភាគតិច 🔲

In this passage you will learn something about the main ethnic minorities in Cambodia.

Vocabulary

អំពី	about, concerning	ទាំងនោះ	all those
ប្រជាជាតិភាគតិច		ដីសណ្ដ	delta
	minority people	មេគុង	Mekong
ចំនួន	number, quantity	ខ្មែរក្រោម	Khmer Krom
លាន	million	សទ្ទេង	voice, accent
ជនជាតិ	people	ជ្រេង(ទៅ)	leaning (towards)
សុទ្ធ	pure	ក្រៅពីនេះ: ...	Apart from ...
ភាគរយ	per cent	យួន	Vietnamese
តិច	small	ចាម	Cham
ព្រៃ	forest, jungle	សញ្ជាតិ	nationality
ភ្នំ	hill	អ្នករកស៊ីធ្វើជំនួញ	
សខាន់	important		businessman,
ព្នង	Pnong (name of		trader
	ethnic minority)	អ្នកជំនួញ	businessman
រ៉ាដេ	Radé (name of	អ្នកនេសាទត្រី	fisherman
	ethnic minority)	ខ្មែរឥស្លាម	Khmer Islam
គុយ	Kuy (name of	ត្បាញ	to weave
	ethnic minority)	សពត់	cloth; a kind of
ខ្មែរលើ	Khmer Leu		skirt
	(Upper Khmer)		

ប្រទេសកម្ពុជា មានចំនួនប្រជាជនប្រហែល ៨ លាននាក់ ជនជាតិខ្មែរសុទ្ធ មានចំនួនប្រហែល ៨០ ភាគរយ។

នៅខេត្តកំពង់ធំ មណ្ឌលគិរី នឹង រតនគិរីមានជនជាតិ
ភាគតិចជាច្រើនដែលរស់នៅតាមព្រៃភ្នំ សំខាន់មាន
ជនជាតិពួង រវែ គុយ ជាដើម ដែលមានឈ្មោះថា
'ខ្មែរលើ'។ ជនជាតិភាគតិចទាំងនោះមានភាសា
សំរាប់ជាតិគេ។

នៅតាមជើសណ្ឌមេកុងមានប្រជាជនខ្មែរមួយចំនួនធំ
រស់នៅទីនោះ ហៅថា 'ខ្មែរក្រោម'។ គេក៏និយាយ
ខ្មែរដែរ តែមានសំឡេងជ្រៀងទៅភាសាវៀតណាម។

ក្រៅពីនេះ ប្រទេសកម្ពុជានៅមានជនជាតិចិន យួន
ចាម ជាដើមដែលមានសញ្ញាតិជាខ្មែរ។ ជនជាតិ
ចិនច្រើនជាអ្នករកស៊ីធ្វើជំនួញ ជនជាតិយួនខ្លះក៏
ជាអ្នកជំនួញដែរ តែភាគច្រើនជាអ្នកនេសាទត្រី
ជនជាតិចាមមានឈ្មោះមួយទៀត ហៅថាខ្មែរឥស្លាម
ច្រើនរកស៊ីនេសាទត្រីនឹងឃ្លាញសំពត់។

14 nou son-ta-gee-a

At the hotel

In this lesson you will learn about:

- days and months
- dates
- taa
- gaa + verb

nou son-ta-gee-a 〔▣▣〕

A: Paul; B: hotel clerk

A:	mee-un bon-dtOOp dtOOm-nay dtay?	មានបន្ទប់ទំនេ ទេ?
B:	baat mee-un.	បាទ មាន។
	loak bom-rong neung nou bpon-maan t'ngai?	លោកបំរុងនឹងនៅ ប៉ុន្មានថ្ងៃ?
A:	meun dtee-ung dtay.	មិនទៀងទេ។
	bpra-hail k'nyom neung nou dol t'ngai sok reu t'ngai sao.	ប្រហែលខ្ញុំនឹងនៅ ដល់ថ្ងៃសុក្រឬថ្ងៃសៅរ៍ ។
B:	loak jong baan bon-dtOOp mee-un maa-seen dtra-jay-uk. reu bon-dtOOp mee-un dong-hul?	លោកចង់បានបន្ទប់ មានម៉ាស៊ីនត្រជាក់ ឬបន្ទប់មានដង្ហាល់?
A:	jong baan bon-dtOOp mee-un	ចង់បានបន្ទប់មាន

	maa-seen dtra-jay-uk.	ម៉ាស៊ីនត្រជាក់
	moo-ay yOOp bpon-maan?	មួយយប់ប៉ុន្មាន?
B:	moo-ay yOOp saam seup dol-laa.	មួយយប់សាមសិបដុល្លា
A:	soum merl bon-dteuch baan dtay?	សូមមើលបន្តិចបានទេ?
B:	baat baan.	បាទ បាន។
	soam un-jerñ dtaam k'nyom.	សូមអញ្ជើញតាមខ្ញុំ ។
	nih bon-dtOOp.	នេះបន្ទប់។
	bpeuñ jeut dtay loak?	ពេញចិត្តទេលោក?

A: *Do you have any free rooms?*
B: *Yes. How many days are you intending to stay?*
A: *I'm not sure. Perhaps I'll stay until Friday or Saturday.*
B: *Do you want a room with air-conditioning or with a fan?*
A: *I want a room with air-conditioning. How much is it a night?*
B: *Thirty dollars a night.*
A: *Could I have a look, please.*
B: *Yes. Please follow me . . . This is the room. Is it satisfactory?*

Vocabulary

bon-dtOOp	room	បន្ទប់
bom-rong	to intend	បំរុង

dtee-ung	to be certain	ទៀង
bpra-hail	perhaps	ប្រហែល
t'ngai sok	Friday	ថ្ងៃសុក្រ
t'ngai sao	Saturday	ថ្ងៃសៅរ៍
maa-seen dtra-jay-uk	air-conditioner	មានម៉ាស៊ីនត្រជាក់
dong-hul	fan	ដង្ហាល់
un-jerñ	please	អញ្ជើញ
dtaam	follow	តាម
bpeuñ jeut	to be pleased	ពេញចិត្ត

Language points

Days and months ⬛⬛

Monday	t'ngai jun	ថ្ងៃចន្ទ
Tuesday	t'ngai ong-gee-a	ថ្ងៃអង្គារ
Wednesday	t'ngai bpOOt	ថ្ងៃពុធ
Thursday	t'ngai bra-hoa-ah	ថ្ងៃព្រហស្បតិ៍
Friday	t'ngai sok	ថ្ងៃសុក្រ
Saturday	t'ngai sao	ថ្ងៃសៅរ៍
Sunday	t'ngai aa-dteut	ថ្ងៃអាទិត្យ

January	may-uk-ga-raa	មករា
February	gom-pay-a	កុម្ភៈ
March	mee-nee-a	មីនា
April	may-saa	មេសា
May	OO-sa-pee-a	ឧសភា
June	mi-to-naa	មិថុនា
July	guk-ga-daa	កក្កដា

August	**say-haa**	សីហា
September	**guñ-nyaa**	កញ្ញា
October	**dto-laa**	តុលា
November	**weutch-ja-gaa**	វិច្ឆិកា
December	**t'noo**	ធ្នូ

Dates

Dates are expressed by the pattern, **t'ngai dtee** + number + month.

t'ngai dtee dop boo-un mee-nee-a   ថ្ងៃទី ១៤ មីនា
14 March

Years are sometimes expressed according to the Buddhist Era, which is 543 years ahead of the A.D. year. Thus 1957 A.D. is 2500 B.E. and 1994 is 2537.

taa

The word **taa** has occurred previously, both as a main verb meaning 'say' (**soam taa m'dorng dtee-ut**) and after verbs of thinking (**yoo-ul taa . . .**) where it can be translated as 'that'. There are several further examples of **taa** following a main verb in the reading passage, where it follows **bprup** ('to tell, inform'), **soo-a** ('to ask') **ch'lar-ee** ('to reply'). Note the difference between 'to tell someone something' (**bprup** someone **taa . . .**) and 'to tell someone to do something' (**bprup** someone **ao-ee . . .**):

gay bprup k'nyom taa aa-may-ri-gung neung moak . . .

គេប្រាប់ខ្ញុំថា អាមេរិកាំងនឹងមក . . .

They told me the Americans were coming to . . .

k'nyom bprup bpra-bpoo-un ao-ee ree-up jom . . .

ខ្ញុំប្រាប់ប្រពន្ធឲ្យរៀបចំ . . .

I told my wife to prepare . . .

gaa + *verb*

In the listening passage you will hear the hotel employee talking about **gaa kwah kaat**. **kwah** and **kaat** are both verbs meaning 'to lack'. When **gaa** is placed in front of a verb it turns it into a noun, so **gaa kwah kaat** means 'lack'. Here are some more examples: **seuk-saa** ('to study'); **gaa seuk-saa** ('studies, education'); **t'wer dom-nar** ('to travel'); **gaa t'wer dom-nar** ('travel').

Pronunciation practice 🔲

A lot of non-Cambodian speakers have difficulty in hearing and producing a distinction between the vowels ៑- and ៑- when they are pronounced with a first series consonant. For the sake of simplicity, they have both been transcribed as **-ai** in the early units. But now it is worth paying some attention to the difference. Listen to the speaker on the tape say (*1*) some words with ៑-, followed by (*2*) words with ៑- and then (*3*) some contrasting pairs of words.

1 ៃដល	ៃខ	ៃត	ៃដរ
'which'	'month'	'but'	'too'
2 ៃដ	ៃថ	ៃថ្ល	ៃថ្ង
'hand'	'Thai'	'expensive'	'day'
3 ៃដរ – ៃដ	ៃត – ៃថ	ៃខ្មរ – ៃថ្ល	
'too' – 'hand'	'but' – 'Thai'	'Khmer' – 'expensive'	

Cambodian voices (4) 🔲

mee-un p'nyee-o klah jeh dtai dtor waa bpee nih bpee nOOh
There are some guests who are always complaining about this and that

On the tape you will hear a Cambodian hotel employee talking about his job and grumbling about some of the guests.

Vocabulary

ភ្ញៀវ	guest	ការខ្វះខាត	lack (n)
ភាគច្រើន	majority	តវ៉ា	to protest, complain
ជនបរទេស	foreigner	ពី	about
អឺរុប	Europe	ជួនកាល	sometimes
ខ្លះ	some	ដើរ	to walk; *here* 'to work'
ជាប់	to be stuck; to stay		
អ្នករកស៊ី	businessman	ស្ទះ	blocked
មិនតិច	not a little, not a few	ជួសជុល	to repair
ចិត្តល្អ	to be kind	មិនទាន់ចិត្ត	'not quick enough for their liking'
យើងខ្ញុំ	we, us		
កំពុង	in the process of	ខឹង	to be angry

ខ្ញុំធ្វើការនៅសន្តាគារនេះបានបី
ឆ្នាំហើយ ។
ភ្ញៀវភាគច្រើនជាជនបរទេស។
មានភ្ញៀវអឺរុបខ្លះ នៅជាប់ជាច្រើនខែ
ព្រោះគេមកធ្វើការនៅស្រុកខ្មែរ។
ក៏មានភ្ញៀវថៃជាអ្នករកស៊ី មិនតិចដែរ។
ភ្ញៀវទាំងនោះ ច្រើនមានចិត្តល្អ ដឹងថាស្រុកយើងខ្ញុំ
កំពុងជួបការខ្វះខាត។ ប៉ុន្តែក៏មានភ្ញៀវខ្លះ
ចេះតែតវ៉ាពីនេះពីនោះ ជួនកាលបើម៉ាស៊ីន
ត្រជាក់ដើរមិនស្រួល ឬ បង្គន់ស្ទះហើយខ្ញុំ
ជួសជុលមិនទាន់ចិត្ត ភ្ញៀវក៏ខឹងនឹងខ្ញុំ។

Questions

When you have listened to and read the passage answer the following questions as a way of practising your writing.

១ ភ្ញៀវភាគច្រើនមកពីណា?

២ មើចប្ទានជាមានភ្លៀវអ្វីបន្ខ្លះនៅឃ្លូរ?
៣ មានភ្លៀវខ្លះចេះតែតវ៉ាពីអ្វី?
៤ បើម៉ាស៊ិនត្រជាក់ដើរមិនស្រួល គាត់ត្រូវធ្វើការអ្វី?
៥ បើគាត់ជួសជុលម៉ាស៊ិនត្រជាក់ ឬ បង្ខន់មិនទាន់ចិត្ត ភ្លៀវក៏ធ្វើអ្វី?

ថ្ងៃទី ១៧ មេសា ▣

This is one Phnom Penh resident's description of how the Khmer Rouge emptied the capital immediately after capturing it.

Vocabulary

ភ្លាម	immediately	
ភ្លាម ៗ នេះ	shortly	
ថ្វរ	please	
	(pronounced **joal**)	
ឆ្លើយ	to reply	
ទិស	direction	
ជើង	north	
អនុញ្ញាត	to allow	

ជឿ (លើ)	to believe (in)	
ពាក្យ	word	
ម្ជឹម្ផ្ញា	to hurry	
ប្រាប់	to inform	
រៀបចាំ	to prepare	
ស្បៀង	supplies, provisions	
អាហារ	food	
ឆ្នាំង	cooking pot	

នៅថ្ងៃទី ១៧ មេសា ១៩៧៥ ប្រហែលរសៀលម៉ោង ២ ពួកទាហានខ្មែរក្រហមមកដល់ផ្ទះខ្ញុំ ប្រាប់ខ្ញុំថា អាមេរិកាំង នឹងមកទម្លាក់គ្រាប់បែកភ្លាម ៗ នេះហើយចូររចេញពីផ្ទះភ្លាម ៤ ខ្ញុំសួរថា លោកត្រូវការឲ្យខ្ញុំទៅកន្លែងណា ? ប៉ុន្មានថ្ងៃទៀត ឲ្យខ្ញុំមកផ្ទះវិញ ? ខ្មែរក្រហមម្នាក់ឆ្លើយថា ចេញតាមទិសខាង ជើងតែ ២ ឬ ៣ ថ្ងៃប៉ុណ្ណោះ គេនឹងអនុញ្ញាតឲ្យមកផ្ទះវិញ ហើយ ៤ ខ្ញុំជឿលើពាក្យដែលពួកនេះនិយាយទាំងអស់ក៏ម្ម៉ិម្ម៉ា ប្រាប់ប្រពន្ធខ្ញុំឲ្យរៀបចំសម្លៀកបំពាក់ នឹងយកស្បៀងអាហារ ខ្លះព្រមទាំងចានឆ្នាំង បន្តិចបន្តួចតែប៉ុណ្ណោះតាមខ្លួន ៤

15 ree-un saa jee-a t'may

Review

This unit reviews material covered in Lessons 11–14.

Exercise 1 🔲

How would you say the following in Cambodian:

1 Could I speak to Tan Kun please?

ខ្ញុំសូមនិយាយនឹងលោកតាន់កុន ប្បានទេ?

2 Please wait a moment. សូមចាំមួយភ្លែត។

3 Hello, Mr Kun. This is Paul. សួស្ដីលោក កុន ខ្ញុំ Paul។

4 When did you arrive in Phnom Penh?

លោកមកភ្នំពេញពីអង្កាល់?

5 Where are you staying now? ឥឡូវនេះសណាក់នៅឯណា?

6 What's this? ស្អីនេះ?

7 What's this called? នេះហៅថាអ្វី?

8 How much a kilo? មួយគីឡូរថ្លៃប៉ុន្មាន?

9 Could you lower the price a little?

ចុះ ថ្លៃបន្តិចបានទេ ?

10 Can I try it? It tastes very good.

លមើលបានទេ? ឆ្ងាញ់ណាស់។

11 I want to change Thai baht into riels.

ខ្ញុំចង់ដួរប្រាទៃជាលុយរៀល។

12 I want to send this letter to America.

ខ្ញុំចង់ផ្ញើសំបុត្រនេះទៅស្រុក
អាមេរិក

13 How much does it cost to send this to England?

នេះផ្ញើទៅស្រុកអង់គ្លេសថ្លៃប៉ុន្មាន?

14 I'd like three 50-riel stamps.

ខ្ញុំសូមតែមប្រិ៍ ៥០ រៀល ៣ សន្លឹក។

15 Do you have any free rooms?

មានបន្ទប់ទំនេរទេ?

16 Does the room have air-conditioning?

បន្ទប់មានម៉ាស៊ីនត្រជាក់ទេ?

17 How much is it per night? មួយយប់ថ្លៃប៉ុន្មាន?

18 Could I have a look, please. សូមមើលបន្តិចបានទេ?

Exercise 2 🔲

Translate the following sentences into English:

១ ស្នែកគាត់នឹងគេឡ្បេហូនម្តងទៀត។

២ សូមនិយាយខ្លាំង ៗ បានទេ?

៣ លោកមកដល់ពីអង្កាល់?

៤ គាត់មកម៉ោងប៉ុន្មាន?

៥ នៅពេល លន់ នល់ ធ្វើស្រេចំការពិបាក។

៦ ពួកអ្នកថ្មីមិនធ្លាប់នឹងធ្វើការហាលថ្ងៃហាលភ្លៀង។

៧ នៅភូមិខ្ញុំ មានអ្នកភូមិជាច្រើនត្រូវស្លាប់បូរប្បុស
ដោយគ្រាប់បែកកប់។

៨ ហេតុនេះខ្ញុំក៏សំរេចចិត្តមករស់នៅក្នុងក្រុងភ្នំពេញ។

៩ មានភ្លៀងៗខ្លះចេះតែករវាំពីនេះពីនោះ។

១០ គេប្រាប់យើងថាត្រូវចេញពីផ្ទះទៅតាមទិសខាងជើង។

16 joo-ul p'dtay-ah

Renting a house

In this lesson you will learn about:
- **goan** versus **k'mayng**
- superlatives, using **bom-pot**
- province names

joo-ul p'dtay-ah 📼

A: Frank; B: Cambodian colleague

A: k'nyom jong rork joo-ul p'dtay-ah   ខ្ញុំចង់រកជួលផ្ទះ
    baan moo-ay.   បានមួយ។
    nou son-ta-gee-a meun s'roo-ul dtay.

                                   នៅសណ្ឋាគារមិនស្រួលទេ។

B: mee-un p'dtay-ah moo-ay som-rup   មានផ្ទះមួយសំរាប់
    joo-ul nou plou tom meun ch'ngai   ជួលនៅផ្លូវធំមិនឆ្ងាយ
    bpee dtee nih bpon-maan dtay.   ពីទីនេះ ប៉ុន្មានទេ។
    m'jah p'dtay-ah jee-a bpoo k'nyom.   ម្ចាស់ផ្ទះ ជាពូខ្ញុំ។

A: mee-un bon-dtOOp bpon-maan?   មានបន្ទប់ប៉ុន្មាន?

B: jee-a wee-laa yaang sa-aat.   ជាវិឡ្ឍាយ៉ាងស្អាត។
    nou baan yaang s'roo-ul loak.

                           នៅបានយ៉ាងស្រួលលោក។

    mee-un bon-dtOOp dayk boo-un   មានបន្ទប់ដេកបួន

bon-dtOOp dtor-dtoo-ul p'nyee-o បន្ទប់ទទួលភ្ញៀវ
moo-ay bon-dtOOp ngoot dteuk bpee

មួយ បន្ទប់ងូតទឹកពីរ
hai-ee neung mee-un soo-un ហើយនឹងមានសួន
som-rup k'mayng layng porng. សំរាប់ក្មេងលេងផង។

A: gay geut t'lai ch'noo-ul moo-ay kai គេគិតថ្លៃឈ្នួលមួយខែ
bpon-maan? ប៉ុន្មាន?

B: moo-ay kai bprum roy dol-laa. មួយខែប្រាំរយដុល្លា។

A: soam dtou merl seun baan dtay?

សូមទៅមើលសិនបានទេ?
B: baan loak jong dtou merl បាន លោកចង់ទៅមើល
nou t'ngai naa? នៅថ្ងៃណា?

A: t'ngai aa-dteut la-or bom-pot. ថ្ងៃអាទិត្យល្អបំផុត។

A: *I'm looking for a house to rent.*
Staying in a hotel isn't convenient.
B: *There's a house for rent on the main road, not far*
from here. The owner is my uncle.
A: *How many rooms does it have?*
B: *It's a lovely villa. You can live there comfortably.*
There are four bedrooms, a living room, two bathrooms
and there is a garden for the children to play in, too.
A: *What is the monthly rent?*
B: *Five hundred dollars a month.*
A: *Can I go and see it first?*
B: *Yes. What day would you like to go?*
A: *Sunday would be best.*

Vocabulary

rork	to look for	រក
joo-ul	to rent	ជួល
s'roo-ul	convenient	ស្រួល

plou (tom)	(main) road	ផ្លូវ (ធំ)
m'jah	owner	ម្ចាស់
bpoo	uncle	ពូ
wee-laa	villa	វិឡា
yaang	way, method, like, as	យ៉ាង
yaang sa-aat	nice	យ៉ាងស្អាត
bon-dtOOp dayk	bedroom	បន្ទប់ដេក
dtor-dtoo-ul	to receive	ទទួល
bon-dtOOp dtor-dtoo-ul p'nyee-o	living room	បន្ទប់ទទួលភ្ញៀវ
bon-dtOOp ngoot dteuk	bathroom	បន្ទប់ងូតទឹក
soo-un	garden	សួន
k'mayng	child(ren)	ក្មេង
t'lai ch'noo-ul	rent	ថ្លៃឈ្នួល
seun	first	សិន
la-or bom-pot	best	ល្អបំផុត

Language points

Children

In the early lessons you met the word **goan** meaning 'child'. **goan** means 'child' in the sense of 'offspring'. When making statements like 'Children nowadays . . .' or 'I have forty-three children in my class', Cambodians use **k'mayng**.

bom-pot

bom-pot can be added after an adjective to make the superlative form.   It has the same meaning as **jee-ung gay**.

Provinces

A full list of province names is given below. Notice that the Cambodian pronunciation of some provinces is quite far removed from the English spelling. The word កំពង់ , incidentally, means 'quay'.

Battambang	ប្រាត់តំបង	**but-dtom-borng**
Kompong Thom	កំពង់ធំ	**gom-bpoo-ung tom**
Kompong Chhnang	កំពង់ឆ្នាំង	**gom-bpoo-ung ch'nung**
Kompong Speu	កំពង់ស្ពឺ	**gom-bpoo-ung speu**
Kompong Cham	កំពង់ចាម	**gom-bpoo-ung jaam**
Kampot	កំពត	**gum-bport**
Kandal	កណ្ដាល	**gon-daal**
Koh Kong	កោះកុង	**goh gong**
Kratié	ក្រចេះ	**gra-jeh**

Mondulkiri	មណ្ឌលគីរី	mOOn-doo-ul-gi-ree
Preah Vihear	ព្រះវិហារ	bpray-ah wi-hee-a
Prey Veng	ព្រៃវែង	bpray-ee wairng
Pursat	ពោធិសាត់	bpoa-saat
Ratanakiri	រតនៈគីរី	roat-ta-na-gi-ree
Siem Reap	សៀមរាប	see-um ree-up
Stung Treng	ស្ទឹងត្រែង	steung dtraing
Svay Rieng	ស្វាយរៀង	swai ree-ung
Takéo	តាកែវ	dtaa-gai-o

Pronunciation practice 🔲

This exercise contrasts the first series pronunciations of the vowels
ເ– and –ា.

កើត – ការ	ដើរ – ដារា
'born' – 'work'	'walk' – Dara (name)
បើ – បាន	ច្រើន – ចាន
'if' – 'can'	'many' – 'plate'

Cambodian voices (5) 🔲

k'nyom neuk s'rok k'mai nah
I miss Cambodia very much

The speaker on the tape fled Cambodia and now lives abroad. Here
he speaks briefly of his escape and his life in a foreign country.

Vocabulary

ក្រោយ	after	ដេញ	to chase (out)
ទាហាន	soldiers	ក្រហម	red
លុកលុយ	to invade	ខ្មែរក្រហម	Khmer Rouge

អស់	completely	ដំណើរ	journey
ផ្សេង	different	ស្នាក់	to stay (temporarily)
លួច	to sneak, steal; do something furtively	ជួយ	to help
		សុំ	to ask for
រត់	to run	សេចក្ដី	matter
ឆ្ពោះទៅ	to, towards	សេចក្ដីអនុញ្ញាត	permission
ចណាយ	to spend (money or time)	រដ្ឋាភិបាល	government
		នឹក	to think of
ជនភៀសខ្លួន	refugee	នឹកស្រុក	to miss one's home country
សំណាងល្អ	good luck		
ជួប	to meet	បំណង	intention
ប្រទះ	to meet, come across	ត្រឡប់ទៅ ...វិញ	to return
		ផង	too

ខ្ញុំចេញពីស្រុកខ្មែរ ជាមួយប្រពន្ធនិងកូនពីរនាក់នៅឆ្នាំ១៩៨២
គឺ បីឆ្នាំក្រោយពេលដែលពួកទាហានយួនចូលលុកលុយស្រុក
ខ្មែរនិងដេញពួកខ្មែរ ក្រហមចេញអស់ទៅ។ គ្រួសារ ខ្ញុំនិង
គ្រួសារ បីផ្សេងទៀតបានលួចរត់ចេញជាមួយគ្នា ឆ្ពោះទៅ
ប្រទេសថៃ យើងខ្ញុំបានចំណាយអស់ពេលប្រហែល ៣០
ថ្ងៃ ទើបបានទៅដល់ជំរំជនភៀសខ្លួននៅប្រទេសថៃ។
ជាសំណាងល្អ យើងខ្ញុំគ្មាន បានជួបប្រទះនិងគ្រោះថ្នាក់អ្វីទេ
នៅដំណើរតាមផ្លូវ។ យើងខ្ញុំស្នាក់នៅក្នុងជំរំជនភៀស
ខ្លួនបាន ៦ ខែ។ ជាសំណាងល្អទៀតប្រពន្ធខ្ញុំមានបង
ប្អូនម្នាក់រកស៊ីនៅប្រទេសអង់គ្លេសបានជួយសុំសេចក្ដី
អនុញ្ញាតិពីរដ្ឋាភិបាលប្រទេសអង់គ្លេស ទើបគ្រួសារ
ខ្ញុំក៏បានមករស់នៅក្នុងប្រទេសអង់គ្លេសទៅ។

ពត្យរខ្មុំមករស់នៅក្នុងប្រទេសអង់គ្លេសបាន ១០
ឆ្នាំហើយ ខ្ញុំនឹកស្រុកខ្មែរណាស់ តែគ្មានបំណងចង់
ត្រឡប់ទៅនៅស្រុកខ្មែរវិញទេ។ កូនខ្ញុំសប្បាយ
នឹងនៅឯនេះណាស់ សព្វថ្ងៃវានិយាយអង់គ្លេស
ចង់ល្អជាងនិយាយខ្មែរផង។

Questions

១ គាត់ចេញពីស្រុកខ្មែរ ជាមួយអ្នកណាខ្លះ?
២ ពួកទាហានយួនចូលដេញពួកខ្មែរក្រហមចេញទៅនៅឆ្នាំអ្វី?
៣ រត់ចេញពីស្រុកខ្មែរ ទៅប្រទេសថៃ
   គាត់បានចំណាយពេលប៉ុន្មានថ្ងៃ?
៤ នៅប្រទេសថៃគ្រូសារ ត្រូវស្នាក់នៅឯណា?
៥ មេីចបានជាគេនៅក្នុងជំរុំជនភៀសខ្លួនបានតែ ២ ខែទេ?
៦ គេនៅស្រុកអង់គ្លេសប៉ុន្មានឆ្នាំហើយ?
៧ គាត់នឹកស្រុកខ្មែរ ទេ?
៨ មេីចបានជាគាត់គ្មានបំណងចង់ត្រឡប់ទៅនៅស្រុក
   ខ្មែរវិញទេ?

ភូមិសាស្ត្រ

This passage is a brief factual description of some of the main geographical features of Cambodia.

Vocabulary

ភូមិសាស្ត្រ	geography	ខាងកើត	east
ភូមិភាគ	region	ខាងត្បូង	south
អាសុីប៉ែកអគ្នេយ៍	South East Asia	ឈូងសមុទ្រ	Gulf of Siam
ប្រទេសលាវ	Laos	សៀម	
ខាងលិច	west	រដូវ	season

រដូវប្រាំង	dry season	ស្ថិត	to be situated
រដូវភ្លៀង	rainy season	ក្បែរ	near to
រដូវរងា	cool season	ទន្លេ	river
(រហូត)ដល់	(all the way through) until	មុខ	face*
ធាតុអាកាស	weather	ទន្លេមេកុង	River Mekong
ក្ដៅ	hot	ទន្លេបាសាក	River Bassac
រាជធានី	capital	ទន្លេសាប	Tonle Sap
នៃ	of		(Great Lake)

* Cambodians refer to the situation of Phnom Penh at the confluence of the Sap, Bassac and Mekong ('four faces'), using the words **boo-un mOOk** because the Mekong appears at that point to have two distinct branches.

ប្រទេសកម្ពុជា ជាប្រទេសមួយនៅភូមិភាគអាស៊ីប៉ែកអាគ្នេយ៍ ។ ខាងជើងមានប្រទេសលាវ ខាងលិចមានប្រទេសថៃ ខាងកើត មានប្រទេសវៀតណាម និងខាងត្បូងជាឈូងសមុទ្រសៀម។ ប្រជាជនខ្មែរភាគច្រើនជាកសិករ។

ប្រទេសកម្ពុជាមានបីរដូវ គឺរដូវប្រាំង រដូវភ្លៀង និងរដូវរងា។ រដូវប្រាំងចាប់តាំងពីខែមីនា រហូតដល់ខែខុសភាព។ រដូវភ្លៀងចាប់តាំងពី ខែមិថុនាដល់ខែវិច្ឆិកា។ រដូវរងាចាប់តាំងពី ខែធ្នូដល់ខែកុម្ភៈ ។ ធាតុអាកាសក្ដៅជាងគេ នៅខែមេសា និងត្រជាក់ជាងគេនៅខែធ្នូ។

រាជធានីនៃប្រទេសកម្ពុជាគឺក្រុងភ្នំពេញ ស្ថិតនៅ ក្បែរទន្លេបួនមុខ។ ទន្លេសំខាន់ជាងគេមាន ទន្លេមេកុង ទន្លេបាសាក និងទន្លេសាប។ សព្វថ្ងៃនេះ ក្រុងភ្នំពេញ មានប្រជាជន ប្រហែលមួយលាននាក់។

17 dar merl saa-ra-moo-un dtee

A visit to the museum

In this lesson you will learn about:

- ao-ee
- *not very* . . .

Cambodia was a popular tourist destination during the French colonial period and, once peace and internal stability are restored, it is likely to become so once again. Indeed, in 1992 there were more than 70,000 visitors, with the famed temples of Angkor Wat a particularly impressive attraction. When visiting temples watch carefully for parts of the temple where you are expected to remove your shoes. Even more importantly, watch where you put your feet when travelling in rural areas: Cambodia has an appallingly high ratio of amputees, and the indiscriminate laying of mines will continue to take its toll on the innocent and unsuspecting for decades.

dar merl saa-ra-moo-un dtee ▮▮

A: Sokha; B: Jill

A:	t'ngai nih Jill jong dtou naa	ថ្ងៃនេះ Jill ចង់ទៅណា
	layng dtay?	លេងទេ?
B:	k'nyom jong dtou merl way-ung.	ខ្ញុំចង់ទៅមើលរាំង។
A:	Jill dail dtou layng	Jill ដែលទៅលេង
	saa-ra-moo-un-dtee	សារមន្ទីរ

nou k'bai way-ung dtay? នៅវៃក្ប្យររាំងទេ?

B: meun dail dtay. មិនៃដលទេ។

A: un-jeung grao-ee bpee merl way-ung

អញ្ជឹង ក្រោយពីមើលរាំង

yerng dtou layng យើងទៅលេង

saa-ra-moo-un-dtee. សារមន្ទីរ។

B: nou k'nong saa-ra-moo-un-dtee នៅក្នុងសារមន្ទីរ

gay ao-ee tort roop dtay? គេឲ្យថតរូបទេ?

A: tort baan ថតបាន

dtai gom bpoa-ul. ៃតកុំពាល់។

bar gay meun ao-ee tort បើគេមិនឲ្យថត

mee-un sor-say uk-sor bprup ao-ee

មានសរ សេរ អក្សរ ព្រាប់ឲ្យ

deung jee-a mOOn. ដឹងជាមុន។

gon-laing nih mee-un dtai កន្លែងនេះមានៃត

bor-ra-dtayh moak layng dtay. បរទេសមកលេងទេ។

nay-uk s'rok meun sou joal jeut អ្នកស្រុកមិនសូវចូលចិត្ត

moak dtee nih dtay. មកទីនេះទេ។

A: *Do you want to go anywhere today, Jill?*
B: *I'd like to go and see the palace.*
A: *Have you ever been to the museum next to the palace?*
B: *No.*
A: *In that case after we've been to the palace we'll go to the museum.*
B: *Can you take photos in the museum?*
A: *Yes. But don't touch (anything). If they don't let you take photos there will be a notice telling you. There are only foreigners who go to visit these places. The locals don't like to very much.*

Vocabulary

dtou layng	to visit	ទៅលេង
way-ung	palace	វាំង
saa-ra-moo-un-dtee	musuem	សារមន្ទីរ
grao-ee bpee	after	ក្រោយពី
ao-ee	to let, allow	ឲ្យ
tort roop	to take a photo	ថតរូប
gom	don't	កុំ
bpoa-ul	to touch	ពាល់
meun soa . . .	hardly; not very	មិនសូវ . . .
bor-ra-dtayh	foreigner	បរទេស
nay-uk s'rok	local people	អ្នកស្រុក

Language points

ao-ee

The word **ao-ee** has occurred a couple of times already. In its most common usage its meaning ranges from 'letting or allowing someone to do something' to 'getting or causing someone to do something', or 'having someone do something':

gay *ao-ee* tort roop dtay?
Do they *let* you take photos?

តើឲ្យថតរូបទេ?

gay meun *ao-ee* joal.
They don't *allow* you to go in.

តើមិនឲ្យចូល។

k'nyom *ao-ee* goa-ut moak t'wer.
I *got* him to come and do it.

ខ្ញុំឲ្យគាត់មកធ្វើ ។

meun sou . . . dtay

In Lesson 4 you met the construction **meun . . . bpon-maan dtay**
meaning 'not very . . .'. **meun sou . . . dtay** has exactly the same
meaning:

> **meun sou tom dtay**
> *not very* big

មិនសូវធំទេ

> **meun sou t'lai dtay**
> *not very* expensive

មិនសូវថ្លៃទេ

Cambodian voices (6)

mee-un buñ-haa tom moo-ay . . . geu reu-ung meen
There is a big problem – that is, mines

In the last passage in this series, a government official talks of
Cambodia's future potential as a tourist destination and the huge
everyday problem of mines.

Vocabulary

សេចក្ដីរីករាយ	happiness	សា	to do again
ឃើញ	to see	ជាថ្មី	anew
សន្តិភាព	peace	ពិតមែន	actually
ចាប់ផ្ដើម	to begin	សភាព	state, condition
ការកសាង	construction	ក្រ	poor

ខ្សត់	poor	មីន	mine (n)
នៅឡើយ	still	សូម្បី	even, including
មុខការ	duty, job	ក្រៅ	outside
ទេសចរណ៍	tourism	រាល់	every
គួរ	ought to, should	តែង	always
ប្រាសាទ	temple, fortress, ruins	មន្ទីរពេទ្យ	hospital
		សុទ្ធតែ	all
អង្គរវត្ត	Angkor Wat	ប្រាត	to lose
មានឈ្មោះល្បី	to be famous	ជើង	foot
ពិភពលោក	world	ម្ខាង	one side
បញ្ហា	problem	ដៃ	arm
ដោះស្រាយ	to solve (a problem)	ជាន់	to step

ខ្ញុំមានសេចក្តីរីករាយណាស់ដែលបានឃើញ
ស្រុកខ្ញុំបានសន្តិភាពហើយកំពុងចាប់ផ្ដើម
ធ្វើការកសាងជាថ្មី ។
ពិតមែនប្រទេសយើងខ្ញុំសព្វថ្ងៃស្ថិតនៅក្នុងសភាព
ក្រខ្សត់នៅឡើយ តែខ្ញុំយល់ថា មុខការទេសចរណ៍
គួរចាប់ផ្ដើមុនគេ ព្រោះកម្ពុជាមានប្រាសាទអង្គរវត្ត
ដែលមានឈ្មោះល្បីក្នុងពិភពលោក មានភ្ញៀវបរទេស
ជាច្រើនចង់មកណាស់។ ប៉ុន្ដែមានបញ្ហាធំមួយដែល
មិនទាន់បានដោះស្រាយ គឺ រឿងមីនដែលមាននៅ
គ្រប់ទីកន្លែង ។ សូម្បីនៅក្រៅភូមិពេញរាល់ថ្ងៃ
តែងមានអ្នកធ្វើស្រែត្រូវស្លាប់ដោយគ្រាប់មីន
ឯមន្ទីរពេទ្យវិញ ក៏ភាគច្រើនសុទ្ធតែជាអ្នករបួស ឬ
ប្រាត់ជើងម្ខាង ឬដៃម្ខាងដោយជាន់លើមីន។

កំប៉ះពាល់មីន

The final reading passage is based on a mine-awareness poster produced by the Mines Advisory Group.

Vocabulary

ប្រយ័ត្ន	watch out, be careful	យកចិត្តទុកដាក់	to pay attention to, be interested in
ថ្ងូរ	*imperative* Do . . .; Please . . .	ប៉ះ	to touch
សញ្ញា	sign	បាត់បង់	to lose

1 ពេលអ្នកចេញក្រៅ
ប្រយ័ត្នចូរមើលសញ្ញាមីន

2 ត្រូវយកចិត្តទុកដាក់មើល
សញ្ញាមីន

3 បើរអ្នកប៉ះមីនអ្នកនឹង
របួស ឬស្លាប់

4 ប្រយ័ត្នពេលចេញក្រៅ
បើអ្នកមិនមើល
សញ្ញាមីនទេ, អ្នក
នឹងបាត់បង់
ជើងដៃ
ឬជីវិត

18 reu-ung k'nyom

The story of my life

The final unit consists of an autobiographical extract in which a Cambodian tells of his childhood and his experiences during the Khmer Rouge period.

To make the passage less daunting, vocabulary has been given at the end of each paragraph. Even so, do not be surprised if each paragraph takes a considerable amount of time. Be prepared to take your time. Take it a paragraph at a time or break it up into even smaller manageable chunks. The very fact that you are now in a position to attempt a piece of Cambodian of this length is in itself indication of the tremendous progress you have made since starting the course.

រឿងខ្ញុំ

១

ខ្ញុំឈ្មោះ តាន់ យុន ស្រុកកំណើតនៅរការាកោង ដែលស្ថិតនៅ តាមដងទន្លេមេគុង មានចម្ងាយ ១៨ គីឡូម៉ែត្រពីក្រុងភ្នំពេញ។ ឪពុកខ្ញុំឈ្មោះ តាន់ ម៉ូរ ម្ដាយឈ្មោះ នាងសុខគី ជាអ្នករកស៊ីធ្វើ ចំការ។ គាត់មានដីជាច្រើនហិកតា សំរាប់ធ្វើដំណាំតាមរដូវ។ តែនៅឆ្នាំ ១៩៦៥ គាត់លក់ចំការចោលរួចបើកហាងលក់របស់ ផ្សេង ៗ នៅផ្សាររការាកោង។

រកាគោង	place name	ដំណាំ	plant
ជង	edge	លក់	to sell
ចម្ងាយ	distance	ចោល	to throw away
ចំការ	market garden, farm	លក់ ... ចោល	to sell up
ដី	land	រួច	then
ហិកតា	hectare	បើក	to open

២

ខ្ញុំមានបងប្រុសម្នាក់នីងបងស្រីម្នួយ ខ្ញុំជាកូនពៅ ខ្ញុំពុកម្ដាយ ខ្ញុំនីងបង ៗ ចូលចិត្តហៅខ្ញុំ 'អាពៅ' ។ យើងខ្ញុំបងប្អូន ទាំងបីនាក់រស់នៅយ៉ាងសុខសប្បាយ តាំងពីក្មេងដល់ធំ ក្រោម ការថែរក្សាយ៉ាងយកចិត្តទុកដាក់របស់ឪពុកម្ដាយ។

កូនពៅ	youngest child	ការថែរក្សា	care (n)
ក្រោម	under		

៣

នៅឆ្នាំ ១៩៦៩ ខ្ញុំបានរៀនចប់មធ្យមសិក្សាទី ២ ថ្នាក់ចុង បំផុតព្រមទាំង ប្រឡងជាប់ 'បាស៊ូ ទី ២' នៅវិទ្យាល័យ ស៊ីសុវត្ថិក្រុងភ្នំពេញ។ ខ្ញុំមានបំណងនីងបន្តការសិក្សា នៅមហាវិទ្យាល័យវេជ្ជពេទ្យនៅដើមឆ្នាំ ១៩៧០ ខាង មុខនោះ ប៉ុន្តែអភ័ព្វពេកណាស់ នៅថ្ងៃទី ១៨ មីនា ១៩៧០ ស្រាប់តែកើតមានរដ្ឋប្រហារ ដឹកនាំដោយលោកឧត្តមសេនីលន់ នល់។

ចប់	to finish	ប្រឡងជាប់	to pass an exam
មធ្យមសិក្សាទី ២	upper secondary school	បាស៊ូ	baccalaureate
ថ្នាក់	class	វិទ្យាល័យ	college, lycée
ចុងបំផុត	top	ស៊ីសុវត្ថិ	Sisowath
ព្រមទាំង	together with	បន្ត	to continue
		ការសិក្សា	education

មហាវិទ្យាល័យ	university	កើត	to happen
វេជ្ជពេទ្យ	medical science	រដ្ឋប្រហារ	*coup d'état*
ដើម	beginning	ដឹក	to lead
អភ័ព្ទ	misfortune	នាំ	to lead
ស្រាប់តែ	suddenly	លោកឧត្ដមសេនីយ៍	General

៤

រដ្ឋប្រហារនេះ បាននាំមកសភាពវឹកវរច្របូកច្របល់
ជាច្រើនខែ សាលារៀនត្រូវបិទទ្វា ប្រជាជននិងកូនសិស្ស
ធ្វើបាតុកម្មមិនឈប់ឈរ ។ ផែនការរៀនសូត្ររបស់ខ្ញុំក៏
ត្រូវរំខាន ហើយបង្ខំចិត្តត្រឡប់មករស់នៅជាមួយឪពុក
ម្ដាយនៅឯស្រុករាកោងវិញទៅ ។

សភាព	state, condition	មិនឈប់ឈរ	endlessly
វឹកវរ	confusion	ផែនការ	plan
ច្របូកច្របល់	mixed up	រៀនសូត្រ	studies
បិទ	to close	រំខាន	to be disturbed
ទ្វា	door	បង្ខំចិត្ត	to force
ប្រជាជន	people	ត្រឡប់ ... វិញ	to return
កូនសិស្ស	student	រស់នៅ	to live
បាតុកម្ម	demonstration		

៥

នៅថ្ងៃទី ១៧ មេសា ១៩៧៥ ពួកខ្មែរក្រហមចូលយក
ក្រុងភ្នំពេញ ដេញអ្នកក្រុងចេញអស់រលីងក្នុងរយៈពេល
បីថ្ងៃ ។ គ្រប់ទិសទីន្លែងឲ្យតែមានផ្លូវ យើញសុទ្ធតែមនុស្ស
ធ្វើដំណើរ ។ នៅផ្លូវរាកោង ក៏មានមនុស្សឆ្លងកាត់
រាប់រយនាក់ក្នុង ១ថ្ងៃ ៗ ។ ទាំងនៅម៉ាត់ទន្លេ
ក៏មានទូកបុ៉កចាយតួចធំរបស់ពួកយួន
ផុ៉តគ្នាដើម្បីធ្វើដំណើរ ទៅកាន់ស្រុកយួនដែរ ។

របីង	completely	មាត់ទន្លេ	river
របៈ	period of time	ទូកប៉ុកចាយ	junk (boat)
គ្រប់ទឹកដន្លែង	everywhere	ផ្តុំគ្នា	gathered together
ឆ្លង	to cross	ដើម្បី	in order to
កាត់	to cut	កាន់	to, towards
រាប់	to count		

๖

មិនយូរប៉ុន្មាន អង្គការខ្មែរក្រហមក៏ចាត់មនុស្សមកដេញ
ពួកអ្នកស្រុករការកាងឲ្យចេញទៅតាំងទីលំនៅថ្មីនៅ
កន្លែងផ្សេង ៗ ដែរ។ គ្រួសារខ្ញុំពេលនោះ ក៏ត្រូវបង្ខំ
ចេញពីរការកោងទៅតាមហ្វូងមនុស្សដែលកំពុងធ្វើដំណើរ
ទៅមុខ។

អង្គការ	organisation	តាម	follow
ចាត់	to assign, arrange	ហ្វូង	crowds, flocks
តាំង	to set up	ធ្វើដំណើរ	to travel
ទីលំនៅ	residence		

๗

ក្រោយបង្អស់ គ្រួសារ ខ្ញុំក៏ត្រូវពួកខ្មែរក្រហមបញ្ជូនទៅ
នៅខេត្តព្រះវិហារ ហើយក្នុងរយៈពេល ៤ ឆ្នាំនោះ
ត្រូវឲ្យផ្លាស់កន្លែងនៅ ពីភូមិមួយទៅភូមិមួយ គឺមុន
ដំបូងនៅភូមិសាមគ្គី រួចភូមិព្រៃវែង ភូមិជាំស្រែ
ភូមិកុងយុង ចុងបង្អស់ ភូមិអន្លុងភ្លួ។

ក្រោយបង្អស់	last of all	ភូមិសាមគ្គី	solidarity village
បញ្ជូន	to send	រួច	then
ផ្លាស់	to move		

៨

ក្នុងរយៈពេល ៤ ឆ្នាំនោះ គ្រួសារខ្ញុំត្រូវស្លាប់
ដោយការ អត់ឃ្លាន នឹង ជម្ងឺគ្រុនចាញ់ សើ្យរតែ
ទាំងអស់ សព្វថ្ងៃនៅសល់តែខ្ញុំហើយនឹង
បងប្រុសខ្ញុំតែពីរនាក់ប៉ុណ្ណោះ ។

ការ អត់ឃ្លាន	starvation	**ទាំង អស់**	completely
ជម្ងឺ	illness	**នៅសល់**	to be left over
គ្រុនចាញ់	fever		

How to write Cambodian

Generally Cambodian letters are written with a single stroke, beginning from the left hand side. This section shows you how the most
common letters are formed.

Lesson 1

Consonants

ន ម ង ញ

វ យ ល ឋ

Vowels

_ា េា េាំ ឹ

ឺ

ៀ ឿ ឹ

Lesson 2

Consonants

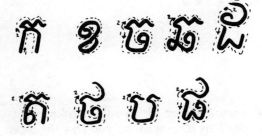

Numbers

Lesson 3

Consonants

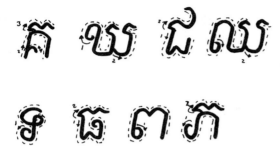

Vowels

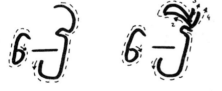

Lesson 4

Subscript consonants

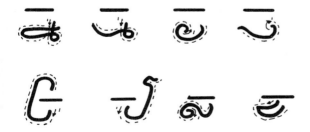

Consonants

Lesson 6

Subscript consonants

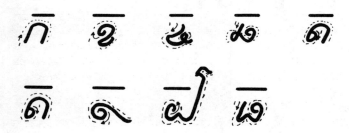

Lessons 6 and 8

Independent vowels

Grammar summary

1 Nouns

There is no distinction in Cambodian between the singular and plural form of a noun. Thus **laan** can mean both 'car' and 'cars'. Usually it is clear from the context whether the speaker is referring to a single item or more than one. Sometimes the word **bpoo-uk** ('group') is used in front of the noun to convey a plural meaning.

bpoo-uk baa-rung meun joal jeut ... Westerners dont like ...

When a specific number is used, it occurs after the noun unless it is a unit of time (e.g. minute, month, year, etc.) or a unit of measure (e.g. metre, kilogram, etc.)

laan boo-un	four cars
bprum t'ngai	five days
dop gee-loa	ten kilos

But when counting people a special 'count-word' or *classifier* has to be used.

2 Classifiers

The classifier **nay-uk** ('person') is used after the number when counting people:

kroo bprum nay-uk	five teachers (teacher-five-person)
borng bpa-oan boo-un nay-uk	four brothers and sisters

Classifiers are used much more extensively in formal Cambodian than in the everyday spoken language. Some other examples of classifiers and the items they are used with are **son-leuk** (stamps, sheets of paper), **darm** (cigarettes, pencils and trees), **ch'bup** (newspapers, letters) and **g'baal** (animals).

3 Pronouns

Cambodian has a much larger number of pronouns than western languages. In Cambodian they can reflect not only gender but also relative age and social status. Cambodians frequently avoid using a word for 'you' and instead address a person by their personal name or by an appropriate kin term. Often pronouns are omitted when the context makes it quite obvious who is being referred to: **n'yum bai hai-ee dtou merl gon**, literally 'eat-rice-already-go-see-movie' means 'when I (we/she/they, etc.) have eaten, I (we etc.) am/are going to a movie.'

4 Adjectives

Adjectives follow the noun they modify:

p'dtay-ah tom	a big house
m'hoap ch'nguñ	tasty food

Adjectives in Cambodian also function as verbs. Thus **tom** means both 'big' and 'to be big' and **ch'nguñ** means both 'tasty' and 'to be tasty'. So the examples above could also be translated as 'the house is big' and 'the food is tasty'. The Cambodian verb **jee-a** 'to be' is not used with adjectives.

5 Verbs

Verbs have a single fixed form. Unlike verbs in European languages, they do not change their form to indicate different tenses or to distinguish between singular and plural. Usually the context is sufficient to indicate whether the verb is referring to events in the past, present or future. When it is necessary to be specific about the time or sequence of actions, Cambodian modifies the verb by adding a word in front or after it.

Future time is indicated by adding the word **neung** in front of the verb:

k'nyom neung dtou p'saa	I shall go to the market.

Past time can be indicated in a number of ways. The word **hai-ee** at the end of the clause or sentence indicates that the action of the verb has been completed:

yerng n'yum bai hai-ee.	We have eaten.

k'nyom t'wer hai-ee.   I have done (it).

The word **baan** in front of the main verb indicates that an action took place in the past:

k'nyom baan dteuñ.   I bought (it).
yerng meun baan dtou.   We did not go.

When **dail** occurs in front of a verb it shows that the action of the verb has occurred on at least one occasion in the past. The negative, **meun dail . . .**, means 'never':

loak dail n'yum m'hoap   Have you ever eaten Cambodian
  k'mai dtay?   food?
k'nyom meun dail dtou   I have never been to France.
  s'rok baa-rung.

The continuous form is indicated by the word **gom-bpOOng** in front of the main verb:

goa-ut gom-bpOOng n'yum bai. He is eating.

The passive is used much less commonly in Cambodian than in English. It is formed using the word **dtrou** in front of the main verb:

goa-ut dtrou (dtom-roo-ut) jup. He was arrested (by the police).

6 Negatives

The negative is formed by placing **meun** in front of the adjective or main verb and, optionally, **dtay** at the end of the phrase or sentence:

meun ch'ngai dtay   not far
meun s'roo-ul dtay   not easy

The negative of **mee-un**, 'to have', is **k'mee-un**:

k'mee-un loo-ee dtay.   (They) don't have any money.

7 Questions

Simple statements can be turned into questions by adding the question word **dtay?** at the end of the sentence:

pee-a-saa k'mai bpi-baak   Cambodian is difficult
pee-a-saa k'mai bpi-baak dtay? Is Cambodian difficult?

Another common question form, similar to the English '. . ., isn't it?', '. . ., aren't they?' is formed by adding **mairn dtay?** at the end of a sentence:

moak bpee p'nOOm bpeuñ mairn dtay?	(You) come from Phnom Penh, don't you?
bprum roy ree-ul mairn dtay?	It's 500 riels, isn't it?

Other useful question words are:

ay/a-way? *('what')*

loak ch'moo-ah ay?	What's your name?
loak t'wer gaa ay?	What (job) do you do?

bpon-maan? *('how much/how many?')*

t'lai bpon-maan?	How much is the price?
aa-yOO bpon-maan ch'num hai-ee?	How old are you?

(ai) naa/(ee)-naa? *('(at) where?')*

nou ai-naa?	Where is (it)?
ree-un nou ai-naa?	Where do (you) study?

Notice that **ai/ee** is dropped in sentences like these:

moak bpee naa?	Where do (you) come from?
loak dtou naa?	Where are you going?

nay-uk naa? *('who?')*

nay-uk naa bprup goa-ut?	Who told him?
yerng dtou joo-up nay-uk naa?	Who are we going to meet?

maych baan jee-a/hait ay baan jee-a *('why?')*

maych baan jee-a loak meun dtou dtay?	Why aren't you going?
hait ay baan jee-a loak jeh pee-a-saa k'mai?	Why can you speak Cambodian?

(bpee) ong-gul? *('when?')*

If a question refers to the future, use **ong-ul?**, and if it refers to the past use **bpee ong-gul?**:

loak moak dol bpee ong-gul?	When did you arrive?
yerng jeuñ ong-gul?	When are we leaving?

8 Word order

The order of words in a sentence tends to follow the pattern *subject + verb + object*. Relative clauses are introduced by the word **dail** ('which', 'where', 'who' etc.):

saalaa dail gay bong-ree-un tai	the school where they teach Thai
borng s'ray dail jee-a kroo	my older sister who is a teacher
p'dtay-ah dail yerng dteuñ	the house which we bought

Key to the exercises

Lesson 1

Exercise 1

1. k'nyom ch'moo-ah ... 2. k'nyom jee-a ... *or* k'nyom jee-a joo-un-jee-ut ...
3. k'nyom moak bpee ... 4. k'nyom jee-a ... 5. k'nyom t'wer gaa nou ...

Exercise 2

1. loak ch'moo-ah ay? 2. loak moak bpee naa? 3. loak t'wer gaa ay?
4. loak t'wer gaa nou ee-naa?

Exercise 3

1. loak ch'moo-ah ay? 2. k'nyom ch'moo-ah som sok. 3. ᴀ: ch'moo-ah
dtra-goal som mairn dtay? ʙ: baat. 4. loak moak bpee naa? 5. k'nyom
moak bpee dtaa-gai-o. 6. loak t'wer gaa nou ee-naa? 7. k'nyom t'wer gaa
nou p'nOOm bpeuñ. 8. k'nyom jee-a bpairt.

Reading passage: Mom

My name is Mom. My family name is Meas. I'm Cambodian. I come from
Battambang. I'm a student. I'm studying English. I study in Phnom Penh.

Exercise 5

nou	nee-ung	mee-un	lee-un	roang
wee-ul	lee-a	wee-a	meeng	meun
mOOn	loo-ee	yoo	moo-ay	yoo-un
yee-ay	lee-ew	nee-a-ree	ni-moo-ay	ni-yee-ay

Exercise 6

(Only the 'full' sentence is given)
1. nee-ung meun mee-un loo-ee. 2. meeng meun nou yoo. 3. nee-ung lee-a nee-ay yoo-un.

Lesson 2

Exercise 1

1. baat (jaa) mee-un bay nay-uk. 2. baat (jaa) mee-un borng s'ray m'nay-uk. 3. borng s'ray ch'moo-ah Jane. 4. borng bproh jee-a bpairt. 5. bpa-oan s'ray ree-un nou lon-dorn.

Exercise 3

1. mee-un borng bpa-oan dtay? 2. baat (jaa) mee-un borng bpa-oan bay nay-uk. 3. k'nyom mee-un borng s'ray m'nay-uk hai-ee neung bpa-oan broh bpee (nay-uk). 4. mee-un roop tort dtay? 5. baat (jaa) nih borng s'ray k'nyom. 6. borng s'ray ch'moo-ah ay? 7. oa-bpOOk t'wer gaa nou ee-naa? 8. m'dai moak bpee naa?

Reading passage: My family

My father was born in China but he lived in Cambodia for a long time. My mother was Cambodian. She came from Kampong Cham province. My parents lived in Phnom Penh for thirty years. I had six brothers and sisters, namely two older sisters, two older brothers one younger brother and one younger sister. Now my parents and five of my brothers and sisters are dead. They died during the Pol Pot period.

Exercise 5

gaa	kao	jao	dtaa	day
jai	bai	bay	boo-un	goan
kaang	taa	kaan	baan	dtaam
doan	gaal	jaam	gaong	baa-ray

Exercise 6

1. 2 5371 2. 2 6049 3. 2 0823 4. 2 7981 5. 2 8457

Exercise 7

1. jaan nou kaang mOOk. 2. dtaa meun mee-un baa-ray. 3. goan meeng dtaam doan. 4. dtaa meun baan jai. 5. ni-yee-ay jeun meun baan.

Lesson 3

Exercise 1

1. mee-un borng bpa-oan bay nay-uk.
2. borng bproh aa-yOO m'pay ch'num hai-ee.
3. bpa-oan s'ray aa-yOO bprum-bpee ch'num hai-ee.
4. oa-bpOOk m'dai mee-un goan boo-un nay-uk.
5. meun mairn dtay. mee-un goan s'ray bpee nay-uk.

Exercise 2

(Here are some possible answers)
1. k'nyom ch'moo-ah Peter. 2. moak bpee Birmingham. 3. aa-yOO m'pay bprum-boo-un ch'num hai-ee. 4. baat mee-un. 5. mee-un borng-bpa-oan bpee nay-uk. 6. baat gaa hai-ee. 7. gaa bpee ch'num hai-ee.

Exercise 3

1. nOOh b'day borng s'ray mairn dtay? 2. meun mairn dtay nOOh borng bproh k'nyom. 3. loak mee-un borng bpa-oan bpon-maan nay-uk? 4. loak mee-un goan bpon-maan nay-uk? 5. k'nyom mee-un goan s'ray m'nay-uk hai-ee neung goan bproh bpee (nay-uk). 6. goan s'ray aa-yOO bpon-maan? ch'moo-ah ay?

Reading passage: My children

I have been married fifteen years. My wife is Thai. She comes from Bangkok. We have lived in this country for about ten years. We have three children. Our daughter is fourteen. She was born in Thailand. Both sons were born in this country. The first one is eleven years old and the second ten.

Exercise 4

geut	goo	goa	jee-a	jeut
joon	joo-up	joo-ay	jee-un	jeu-a
dtee-a	dteuñ	dtoo	dtou	dtee-ut

dteu-un	tee-a-nee-a	toop	bpeut	bpee
bpee	bpoo-uk	bpi-baak	pee-uk	poom

Exercise 5

1. dtaa geut meun dtou. 2. dtou dtaam dtook bpi-baak. 3. joo-un gaal
dtou poom bpi-baak. 4. goan meun moak ree-un.

Exercise 6

goo-ich	kaat	koa-ich	geut	goo-a	ngoot
jort	jorp	jaak	baat	pee-uk	pee-up
doa-ich	dtoa-ich	roop	mOOk	ree-uk	ree-ich

Lesson 4

Exercise 1

(Here are some possible answers)
1. k'nyom ni-yee-ay baan bon-dteuch bon-dtoo-ich. 2. ree-un (pee-a-saa
k'mai) nou s'rok tai. 3. meun yoo dtay. 4. mee-un kroo k'mai bong-ree-
un. 5. meun bpi-baak bpon-maan dtay. 6. sor-say (uk-sor k'mai) meun
baan dtay.

Exercise 2

2. borng bproh ni-yee-ay pee-a-saa baa-rung baan bon-dteuch bon-dtoo-ich.
3. borng bproh ni-yee-ay pee-a-saa ong-klayh baan bon-dteuch bon-dtoo-
ich. 4. borng bproh ni-yee-ay pee-a-saa ong-klayh baan la-or. 5. borng
bproh sor-say pee-a-saa ong-klayh baan la-or. 6. borng bproh sor-say pee-
a-saa ong-klayh baan s'roo-ul. 7. borng bproh merl aan pee-a-saa ong-
klayh baan s'roo-ul. 8. m'dai k'nyom merl aan pee-a-saa ong-klayh baan
s'roo-ul.

Exercise 3

1. loak jeh ni-yee-ay pee-a-saa ong-klayh reu dtay? 2. k'nyom ni-yee-ay
pee-a-saa baa-rung meun baan dtay *or* k'nyom meun jeh ni-yee-ay pee-a-
saa baa-rung dtay. 3. loak s'dup baan dtay? 4. soam taa m'dorng dtee-ut.
5. k'nyom ni-yee-ay pee-a-saa k'mai baan bon-dteuch bon-dtoo-ich bon-
dtai k'nyom sor-say meun baan dtay.

Reading passage: Learning Cambodian

Before going to work in Cambodia Sally has to study Cambodian. In this country there is only one school where they teach Cambodian. Sally goes to this school two hours a day. She learns to speak, read and write the Cambodian alphabet. The teacher is Cambodian. He comes from Kompong Thom, but he has lived in this country for a long time. At first Cambodian was not easy to learn. Sally could not understand the teacher. It was difficult to speak. But after studying for two or three months Sally can speak well, read easily and write a little. Now Sally thinks that Cambodian is not so difficult.

Exercise 5

naa	naai	saap	sok	soam
soo-un	sorng	see-um	haa	haang
hok seup	hoa	hoo-ah	hao	laan
aich	aa-yOO	aa-gaah	aa-gee-a	saa-laa

Exercise 6

k'nee-a	k'mee-un	kree-a	kroo-a-saa	t'may
ch'ree-up	ch'rOOng	t'wee-a	bprorm	s'roo-ul
bproo-ay	k'moo-ay	k'nong	klaa	klaich
kloo-un	klee-un	ch'ngai	ch'num	ch'maa

Exercise 7

1. kroo moak saa-laa ree-un. 2. dtaa sok bproo-ay yoo. 3. kroo-a-saa meun bprorm moak.

Lesson 5

Exercise 1

1. loak ch'moo-ah ay? 2. ch'moo-ah dtra-goal ay? 3. loak moak bpee naa? 4. moak bpee s'rok ay? *or* moak bpee s'rok naa? 5. moak bpee kait ay? *or* moak bpee kait naa? 6. t'wer gaa ay? 7. t'wer gaa nou ai-naa? 8. t'wer gaa nou ai nOOh yoo dtay? 9. gaa hai-ee reu nou? 10. b'day t'wer gaa ay? 11. bpra-bpoo-un t'wer gaa dtay? 12. gaa bpon-maan ch'num hai-ee? 13. mee-un goan hai-ee reu nou? 14. mee-un goan bpon-maan nay-uk? 15. mee-un goan bproh bpon-maan nay-uk? 16. loak aa-yOO bpon-maan?

17. b'day aa-yOO bpon-maan? 18. goan bproh dtee moo-ay aa-yOO bpon-maan? 19. mee-un borng bpa-oan dtay? 20. borng s'ray mee-un goan hai-ee reu nou? 21. jeh ni-yee-ay pee-a-saa k'mai reu dtay? 22. loak ni-yee-ay pee-a-saa ong-klayh baan la-or 23. k'nyom ni-yee-ay pee-a-saa k'mai baan bon-dteuch bon-dtoo-ich. 24. ree-un pee-a-saa ong-klayh yoo dtay? 25. nay-uk naa bong-ree-un pee-a-saa ong-klayh? 26. kroo loak moak bpee naa?

Exercise 2

nou	meun	yoo	baan	dtou
ree-un	aa-yOO	ch'num	nee-ung	loo-ee
bay	bai	jee-ung	bpee	k'mee-un
bprum	mee-un	moo-ay	boo-un	goan
moak	soam	k'nong	lee-a	ni-yee-ay
dtaam	geut	dorng	haang	s'roo-ul
klaich	hao	klee-un	poom	t'may
bpi-baak	dtoa-ich	pee-uk	bpoo-uk	kroo

Lesson 6

Exercise 1

1. dtou woa-ut p'nOOm t'lai bpon-maan? 2. dtou son-taa-gee-a ma-noa-rom t'lai bpon-maan? 3. dtou p'saa oa-reu-say t'lai bpon-maan? 4. dtou p'saa t'may t'lai bpon-maan? 5. dtou staad oa-lum-bpeek t'lai bpon-maan?

Exercise 2

1. staad oa-lum-bpeek skoa-ul dtay? 2. dtou son-taa-gee-a ma-noa-rom t'lai bpon-maan? 3. m'roy ree-ul t'lai nah. 4. meun ch'ngai bpon-maan dtay. 5. bpait seup ree-ul baan dtay?

Exercise 3

2. t'lai nah toa-um-ma-daa k'nyom dtou dtai sai seup ree-ul dtay. 3. t'lai nah toa-um-ma-daa k'nyom dtou dtai saam seup ree-ul dtay.

Exercise 4

p'gaa	ch'goo-ut	s'kor	m'kaang	l'kaon
k'jay	b'day	b'doa	p'daah	m'dai
s'dai	s'dum	s'taan	s'teut	g'baal
ch'baa	t'baañ	dt'beut	dt'boang	l'bay

Exercise 5

bar	dar	larng	ler	yerng
merl	jayk	dayk	day	gay
gayng	layng	bpayl	joh	lOOh
p'darm	j'rarn	brar	s'rok	k'nyom

Exercise 6

A: Where are you going?
B: I'm going to work.
A: Where do you work?
B: I work in a school. I'm a teacher.
A: Where's the school?
B: The school is near the Olympic Stadium.
A: What do you teach?
B: I teach Chinese.
A: Is Chinese difficult?
B: Chinese is difficult to write but it's easy to speak.

Lesson 7

Exercise 1

1. baan. 2. ch'nguñ. 3. baan. 4. joal jeut. 5. heul.

Exercise 2

1. k'nyom n'yum m'hoap heul meun baan dtay. 2. som-lor m'joo meun ch'nguñ bpon-maan dtay. 3. soam yoak dtaa-raang m'hoap moak merl. 4. soam bai chaa sai-ich moa-un moo-ay jaan hai-ee neung bee-a moo-ay dorp.

Exercise 3

dteuk	neung	deung	geu
dtai	dail	k'mai	mairn
dai	tai	t'lai	t'ngai

Exercise 4

1. chicken 2. shrimp 3. pork 4. beef 5. crab

Exercise 5

2 and 4

Lesson 8

Exercise 1

1. soam bee-a moo-ay dorp. 2. bee-a nih meun dtra-jay-uk dtay mee-un bee-a dtra-jay-uk dtay? 3. soam goa-goa goa-laa moo-ay dtee-ut. 4. k'nyom n'yum meun baan dtay pa-aim bpayk. 5. soam geut loo-ee.

Exercise 2

1. Gentlemen 2. Toilet 3. Ladies
(Note that the word for Ladies is not **s'ray** but **s'dtray** – a more formal term.)

Exercise 3

A: bong-aim k'mai pa-aim bpayk reu dtay?
B: dtay ch'nguñ nah.
A: loak n'yum dtay?
B: dtay k'nyom cha-ait hai-ee.
A: nee-ung nee-ung soam geut loo-ee.
C: bprum roy hok seup ree-ul.

Reading passage: Cambodian food

Many Cambodians think that English food has no flavour. They say that Cambodian food is tastier. But in England there aren't any Cambodian restaurants. So Cambodians in England like to go and eat in Chinese or

Thai restaurants. As for English people, when they go to Cambodia they mostly cannot eat Cambodian food. They say it is too spicy or too sweet or too sour.

Exercise 4

tom	gom-bport	kom	p'nOOm	nOOm
jum	ch'num	t'num	noa-um	roa-um
gom	k'nyom	dom	dtung	dtay-ung
m'hoap	la-or	sa-aat		

Exercise 5

bong	nay-uk	nah	jong	ong-klayh
m'nay-uk	s'dup	s'koa-ul	dop	bot
dtrong	chOOp	(meun) dtoa-un	ch'nguñ	bong-goo-un
sai-ich				

Exercise 6

Goy comes from a small village in Siem Reap. His parents are farmers. He has two brothers and sisters. His elder sister is married and has three children, namely a daughter and two sons. Her sister's husband comes from Svay Rieng. He is a teacher at the school in Goy's village. His younger brother is nineteen. He doesn't want to be a farmer.

Lesson 9

Exercise 1

1. k'nyom jong nai noa-um loak So-pee-up ao-ee s'koa-ul borng s'ray k'nyom. 2. . . . goan bproh k'nyom. 3. . . . bpoo-uk maak k'nyom ch'moo-ah Som Sok. 4. . . . m'dai k'nyom. 5. . . . kroo k'nyom.

Exercise 2

1b 2d 3a 4c

Exercise 3

p'dtay-ah	joh	lOOh
jeh	nih	bpray-ah
goh	bproo-ah	nOOh

Lesson 10

Exercise 1

1. staad oa-lum-bpeek s'koa-ul dtay? 2. dtou p'saa oa-reu-say t'lai bpon-maan? 3. meun ch'ngai bpon-maan dtay toa um-ma-daa k'nyom dtou dtai haa seup ree-ul dtay. 4. bot dtou kaang ch'wayng hai-ee dtou mOOk dtrong. 5. soam joon k'nyom dtou woa-ut p'nOOm. 6. soam yoak dtaa-raang m'hoap moak merl. 7. k'nyom n'yum m'hoap heul meun baan dtay. 8. k'nyom jong baan goa-gaa goa-laa moo-ay dorp hai-ee neung bai chaa sai-ich moa-un moo-ay jaan. 9. ch'nguñ dtay? 10. meun ch'nguñ dtay pa-aim bpayk. 11. n'yum meun baan dtay cha-ait hai-ee. 12. k'nyom meun klee-un dtay. 13. soam dtoah bong-goo-un nou ee-naa? 14. soam geut loo-ee. 15. soo-a s'day sok sa-bai jee-a dtay? 16. k'nyom dtrayk-or dail baan s'koa-ul loak. 17. maych baan jee-a loak jeh k'mai? 18. k'nyom dail t'wer gaa nou jOOm-rOOm nou s'rok tai. 19. bpayl nOOh k'nyom mee-un bpoo-uk maak k'mai j'rarn.

Exercise 2

j'rarn	bprup	dail	dteuk	m'hoap
joh	dayk	bproo-ah	k'nyom	s'dum
nay-uk	m'dai	sa-aat	dop	b'day
p'dtay-ah	oa-bpOOk	ai-naa	gay	bpon-maan
mairn	ch'nguñ	jeh	reu	see
t'ngai	sai-ich	p'nOOm	ay-lou	chOOp

Lesson 11

Exercise 1

1. k'nyom soam ni-yee-ay neung loak tun kOOn baan dtay? 2. k'nyom soam ni-yee-ay neung nay-uk s'ray mee-ah sOO-jee-ut baan dtay? 3. k'nyom soam ni-yee-ay neung loak bpou dtee-gee-a baan dtay? 4. k'nyom soam ni-yee-ay neung nay-uk s'ray geum mom baan dtay?

Exercise 2

1. maong dop bpee kwah bprum nee-a-dtee (hai-ee). 2. maong bprum gon-lah (hai-ee). 3. maong bprum moo-ay neung m'pay bprum nee-a-dtee (hai-ee). 4. maong dop (hai-ee). 5. maong bpee neung dop bprum nee-a-dtee (hai-ee).

Exercise 3

1. moak s'rok ong-klayh bpee ong-gul? 2. dtou t'wer gaa maong bpon-maan? 3. dtou s'rok k'mai ong-gul? 4. maong bpon-maan hai-ee? 5. yerng joo-up k'nee-a ong-gul?

Cambodian voices (1)

My name is Sokha. I work as a typist in an office in Phnom Penh. I work eight hours a day. I start work in the morning at half-past seven and I leave work in the evening at half-past five. At midday, from twelve o'clock until two o'clock in the afternoon, it is a time for rest.

My salary is not enough to support my family. It is just enough for me. That is why I have to take the opportunity to work extra in the evenings in a restaurant, right through until midnight, before I return home.

Lesson 12

Cambodian voices (2)

My name is Goy. I'm sixty-three. I've lived in this village since I was born. During the Lon Nol period it was very difficult to farm. The Americans were always dropping bombs on the fields, killing quite a few people. In the Pol Pot period lots of people from Phnom Penh came to live in my village. All these city people they called 'new people'. As for us, they called us 'old people'.

Most of the new people who came to stay in my village were not used to working out in the open exposed to the sun and rain like us. Before long they became ill and even died, because at that time there were no doctors and no medicine. When the Vietnamese soldiers came, all the city people left my village and went back to Phnom Penh.

Markets

In every province, district, town and village in Cambodia there is a market, large or small, for traders to sell and exchange their various goods. In Phnom Penh the most famous market is the New Market or Big Market. Apart from this, there is the Central Market, the Old Market, the Olympic Market and the O Russei Market.

In all these markets they sell various goods. There are fruits, vegetables, fish, meat, clothes, books, household utensils.

Before buying anything we can bargain the price. But once we have handed over the money, if we want to get our money back it will be very difficult.

Lesson 13

Cambodian voices (3)

I come from Stung Treng. I have been living in Phnom Penh, working as a cyclo driver for eighteen months. I used to be a farmer, but farming in my district now is very difficult. It is very dangerous because there are mines all over the place. In my village there are many villagers who have been killed or injured by mines. Now hardly any of the villagers dares to walk far from the village. That's why I decided to bring my wife and children to live in Phnom Penh.

Exercise 1

១. ប្រាន ២. ស្ទើតែ ៣. ស្ទើតែ ៤. ត្រូវ

Exercise 2

1. som-bot nih p'nyar dtou s'rok ong-klayh t'lai bpon-maan? 2. k'nyom jong p'nyar som-bot nih dtou dtaam ga-bul hoh. 3. k'nyom soam dtaim m'roy ree-ul bay son-leuk hai-ee neung dtaim haa-seup ree-ul bpee son-leuk. 4. moo-ay dol-laa bpon-maan ree-ul? 5. k'nyom jong doa loo-ee dol-laa jee-a loo-ee ree-ul.

Ethnic minorities

Cambodia has a population of approximately eight million people. Approximately eighty per cent of these are pure Khmer people.

In Kompong Thom, Mondulkiri and Ratanakiri there are many minority peoples who live in the jungles and mountains. The important (groups) are the Pnong, Radé, Kuy, who are known as the Khmer Leu (Upper Khmer). All these peoples have their own languages.

In the Mekong Delta there is a large number of Khmer people called Khmer Krom (Lower Khmer). They speak Cambodian, too, but their accent is similar to Vietnamese.

Apart from these, Cambodia has Chinese, Vietnamese and Cham people who have Cambodian nationality. Most Chinese people are businessmen. Some Vietnamese are businessmen, too, but the majority are fishermen. The Chams have another name, They are are called 'Khmer Islam'. Most earn a living from fishing and weaving.

Lesson 14

Cambodian voices (4)

I have worked in this hotel for three years. Most of the guests are foreigners. There are some Europeans who stay for many months because they have come to work in Cambodia. And there are quite a lot of Thai guests, who are businessmen, too. Most of the guests are nice. They know that our country is facing shortages. But there are some guests who are always complaining about this or that. Sometimes, if the air-conditioner isn't working properly or the toilet is blocked up and I don't repair it quickly enough for their liking, they get angry with me.

On 17 April

On 17 April 1975 at about two o'clock in the afternoon, Khmer Rouge soldiers came to my house and told me that the Americans were going to drop bombs immediately and to please leave the house at once. I asked them where they wanted me to go and how many days before they would let me return. One of the Khmer Rouge replied that we should go northwards for just two or three days and then they would allow us to return to our homes. I completely believed what they said and hurried to tell my wife to prepare clothes and provisions as well as pots and pans.

Lesson 15

Exercise 1

The answers are given in Cambodian script opposite.

Exercise 2

1. Tomorrow he will telephone again. 2. Could you speak loudly, please? 3. When did you arrive? 4. What time is he coming? 5. Farming was difficult during the Lon Nol period. 6. The 'new people' were not used to working exposed to the sun and rain. 7. In my village many villagers have been killed or wounded by mines. 8. This is why I decided to come and live in Phnom Penh. 9. Some guests are always complaining about this and that. 10. They told us we had to leave our house and go north.

Lesson 16

Cambodian voices (5)

I left Cambodia with my wife and two children in 1982, that is, three years after the time when Vietnamese soldiers invaded Cambodia and chased away all the Khmer Rouge. My family and three other families sneaked away together towards Thailand. We spent altogether about thirty days before we came to a refugee camp in Thailand. It was good luck that we did not meet with any danger on the way. We stayed in the refugee camp for six months. It was good luck again that my wife had a brother working in England who helped to ask for permission from the British government and then my family came to live in England.

Now I have been living in England for ten years I miss Cambodia a lot but I have no wish to go back and live there. My children are very happy living here. Now they speak English even better than Cambodian, too.

Geography

Cambodia is a country in South East Asia. To the north is Laos, to the west Thailand, to the east Vietnam and to the south the Gulf of Siam. The majority of Cambodian people are farmers.

Cambodia has three seasons – a dry season, a rainy season and a cool season. The dry season begins in March and continues until May. The rainy season begins in June and continues until November. The cool season begins in December and goes on until February. The weather is hottest in April and coolest in December.

The capital of Cambodia is Phnom Penh. It is situated on the bank of the Mekong. The most important rivers are the Mekong, Bassac and Sap. Today Phnom Penh has a population of about a million people.

Lesson 17

Cambodian voices (6)

I'm very pleased that my country has peace and is beginning to rebuild. In fact our country today is in a state of poverty. But I think that tourism should be a priority because Cambodia has the temples of Angkor Wat which are famous throughout the world and very many foreigners want to come. But there is one problem which has not been solved yet, that is the problem of mines, which are everywhere. Even (just) outside Phnom Penh every day there are always farmers killed by mines. As for the hospitals, the majority (in them) are those wounded or who have lost a leg or an arm by stepping on a mine.

Don't touch mines

1 When you go out, beware and look for signs of mines.
2 You must be aware and look for signs of mines.
3 If you touch a mine you will be wounded or killed.
4 Watch out when you go out. If you do not look out for signs of mines you will lose a leg, an arm or your life.

English–Cambodian glossary

able (can)	baan	ប្រាន
about (approximately)	bpra-hail	ប្រហែល
(concerning)	bpee; om-bpee	ពី; អំពី
above	ler	លើ
abroad	grao bpra-dtayh	ក្រៅប្រទេស
accept	dtor-dtoo-ul	ទទួល
accident	kroo-ah t'nuk	គ្រោះថ្នាក់
according to	dtaam	តាម
ache	cheu	ឈឺ
headache	cheu g'baal	ឈឺក្បាល
stomach ache	cheu bpoo-ah	ឈឺពោះ
address	dtee 100m-nou	ទីលំនៅ
advantage	bpra-yaoch	ប្រយោជន៍
advise	s'nar	ស្នើ
aeroplane	g'bul hoh;	កប៉ាល់ហោះ;
	yoo-un hoh	យន្តហោះ
afraid	klaich	ខ្លាច
after	grao-ee	ក្រោយ
afternoon (early)	ra-see-ul	រសៀល
(late)	l'ngee-ich	ល្ងាច
afterwards	grao-ee moak	ក្រោយមក

again	dtee-ut; m'dorng dtee-ut	ទៀត; ម្ដងទៀត
age	aa-yOO	អាយុ
ago	mOOn	មុន
agree (with, to)	yoo-ul bprorm (neung)	យល់ព្រម(នឹង)
air	aa-gaah	អាកាស
air-conditioner	maa-seen dtra-jay-uk	ម៉ាស៊ីនត្រជាក់
alcohol (liquor)	s'raa	ស្រា
all	dtay-ung oh	ទាំងអស់
almost	jeut (neung)	ជិត(នឹង)
along	dtaam	តាម
already	hai-ee	ហើយ
also	dai	ដែរ
always	jee-a neuch; jee-a dor-raap	ជានិច្ច; ជាជរាប
America	sa-haa roa-ut a-may-reuk	សហារដ្ឋអមេរិក
amount	jom-noo-un	ចំនួន
and	neung	នឹង
Angkor Wat	ung-gor woa-ut	អង្គរវត្ត
angry	keung	ខឹង
animal	sut	សត្វ
announce	bpra-gaah	ប្រកាស
appropriate (adj)	som-rOOm	សមរម្យ
arm	dai	ដៃ
army	gong dtoa-up	កងទ័ព
arrange	jut jaing; ree-up jom	ចាត់ចែង; រៀបចំ
arrest (v)	jup	ចាប់
arrive	dol	ដល់
ask (a question)	som soo-a	សុំសួរ
ask (for something)	som	សុំ

asleep	**dayk loo-uk**	ដេកលក់
at	**nou**	នៅ
bad	**aa-krok; koa-ich**	អាក្រក់; ខូច
bag	**tong**	ថង់
bank	**tor-nee-a-gee-a**	ធនាគារ
bargain (v)	**dtor t'lai**	តថ្លៃ
bathe	**ngoot dteuk**	ងូតទឹក
bathroom	**bon-dtOOp dteuk**	បន្ទប់ទឹក
beat (v)	**wee-ay**	វាយ
beautiful	**sa-aat; la-or**	ស្អាត; ល្អ
because	**bproo-ah**	ព្រោះ
bed	**grair dayk**	គ្រែដេក
bedroom	**bon-dtOOp dayk**	បន្ទប់ដេក
before	**mOOn**	មុន
begin	**jup p'darm**	ចាប់ផ្ដើម
behind	**kaang grao-ee**	ខាងក្រោយ
believe	**jeu-a**	ជឿ
below	**kaang graom**	ខាងក្រោម
best	**la-or jee-ung gay**	ល្អជាងគេ
better	**la-or jee-ung**	ល្អជាង
between	**ra-wee-ung**	រវាង
bicycle	**gong; ror-dtayh gong**	កង់; រទេះកង់
big	**tom**	ធំ
black	**bpoa-a k'mao**	ពណ៌ខ្មៅ
blood	**chee-um**	ឈាម
blue	**bpoa-a kee-o**	ពណ៌ខៀវ
board (n)	**g'daa**	ក្ដារ

boat	dtook	ទូក
body	dtoo-a	ត្ងួ
born (to be born)	gart	កើត
both	dtay-ung bpee	ទាំងពីរ
bottle	dorp	ដប
boy	bproh; k'mayng bproh	ប្រុស; ក្មេងប្រុស
bread	nOOm-bpung	នំប៉័ង
break (v) (things)	baik	បែក
breakfast	bai bpreuk	ប្រាយព្រឹក
bridge	spee-un	ស្ពាន
bring	yoak . . . moak	យក . . . មក
broken	koa-ich	ខូច
brother (elder)	borng bproh	បងប្រុស
(younger)	bpa-oan bproh	ប្អូនប្រុស
brothers and sisters	borng bpa-oan	បងប្អូន
brown	bpoa-a t'naot	ពណ៌ផ្ទោត
bucket	tung	ថាំង
Buddha	bpray-ah bpOOt	ព្រះពុទ្ធ
Buddhism	bpOOt-ta-saa-s'naa	ពុទ្ធសាសនា
buffalo	gra-bay	ក្របី
build	song; gor saang	សង់; កសាង
bus	laan ch'noo-ul	ឡានឈ្នួល
business	jOOm-noo-uñ	ជំនួញ
businessman	nay-uk jOOm-noo-uñ	អ្នកជំនួញ
busy	ra-woo-ul	រវល់
but	dtai; bpon-dtai	តែ; ប៉ុន្តែ
buy	dteuñ	ទិញ
by	dao-ee	ដោយ

cage	dtrOOng	ទ្រុង
calendar	bra-gra-day-dtin	ប្រក្រតិទិន
call	hao	ហៅ
Cambodia	gum-bpOO-jee-a; s'rok k'mai	កម្ពុជា; ស្រុកខ្មែរ
Cambodian	k'mai	ខ្មែរ
camera	maa-seen tort roop	ម៉ាស៊ីនថតរូប
camp (army, refugee)	jOOm-rOOm	ជំរំ
can (v)	baan	បាន
canal	bpra-lai	ប្រឡាយ
candle	dtee-un	ទៀន
cannot...	... meun baan dtay	...មិនបានទេ
capture	jup	ចាប់
car	laan	ឡាន
card (playing)	bee-a	បៀ
care for	tai ray-uk-saa	ថែរក្សា
careful	bpra-yut	ប្រយ័ត្ន
carry (in the hands)	gun	កាន់
(on the back or shoulders)	lee	លី
cart	ror-dtayh	រទេះ
cat	ch'maa	ឆ្មា
catch (v)	jup	ចាប់
cause (n)	hait	ហេតុ
cause (v)	ao-ee; bon-daal	ឲ្យ (អោយ); បណ្ដាល
ceremony	bpi-tee	ពិធី
certain	jee-a bpraa-got	ជាប្រាកដ
certainly, of course	neung hai-ee	ហ្នឹងហើយ

chair	**gao-ay**	កៅអី
chance	**oa-gaah**	ឱកាស
change (n)	**gaa bprai bproo-ul**	ការប្រែប្រួល
change (v)	**plah p'doa**	ផ្លាស់ប្តូរ
chase (away)	**dayñ jeuñ**	ដេញចេញ
chat (v)	**ni-yee-ay layng**	និយាយលេង
cheap	**taok**	ថោក
cheat (v)	**baok**	បោក
chest (body)	**ok**	អុក
chicken	**moa-un**	មាន់
child (one's own)	**goan**	កូន
child	**k'mayng**	ក្មេង
China	**jeun**	ចិន
cholera	**aa-son-na-roak**	អាសន្នរោគ
choose	**rerh**	រើស
chopsticks	**jong-geuh**	ចង្កឹះ
cigarette	**baa-ray**	បារី
cinema	**roang gon**	រោងកុន
city	**dtee grong**	ទីក្រុង
class	**t'nuk**	ថ្នាក់
clean	**sa-aat**	ស្អាត
clear	**ch'bah**	ច្បាស់
clever	**bpraach-ñaa**	ប្រាជ្ញា
clock	**nee-a-li-gaa**	នាឡិកា
close, shut	**beut**	បិទ
close, near	**jeut**	ជិត
clothes	**kao-ao**	ខោអាវ
cockroach	**gon-laat**	កន្លាត

coconut	**doang**	ដូង
coffee	**gaa-fay**	កាហ្វេ
cold (adj)	**ra-ngee-a**	រងា
colour	**bpoa-a**	ពណិ
come	**moak**	មក
comfortable	**s'roo-ul**	ស្រួល
compare	**bpree-up tee-up**	ប្រៀបធៀប
complain	**dtor waa**	តវ៉ា
contented	**sop-bai jeut**	សប្បាយចិត្ត
continue	**dtor**	ត
cook (v)	**t'wer bai**	ធ្វើបាយ
cool	**dtra-jay-uk**	ត្រជាក់
copy (v)	**jom-lorng**	ចម្លង
correct	**dtrou**	ត្រូវ
cost	**t'lai**	ថ្លៃ
cough	**ga-ork**	ក្អក
count	**roa-up**	រាប់
country	**bpror-dtayh; s'rok**	ប្រទេស; ស្រុក
countryside	**s'rok s'rai**	ស្រុកស្រែ
cow	**goa**	គោ
crab	**g'daam**	ក្ដាម
crazy	**ch'goo-ut**	ឆ្កួត
crippled	**bpi-gaa**	ពិការ
crops	**dom-num**	ដំណាំ
crowded	**jong-ee-ut**	ចង្អៀត
cry (tears)	**yOOm**	យំ
cup	**bpairng**	ពែង
cupboard	**dtoo**	ទូ

cut (v)	**gut**	កាត់
cyclo	**see-kloa**	ស៊ីក្លូ
dance (n)	**ra-bum**	របាំ
dance (v)	**roa-um**	រាំ
danger	**kroo-ah t'nuk**	គ្រោះថ្នាក់
dare to	**hee-un**	ហ៊ាន
daughter	**goan s'ray**	កូនស្រី
day	**t'ngai**	ថ្ងៃ
dead	**s'lup**	ស្លាប់
decide	**som-raich jeut**	សំរេចចិត្ត
delicious	**ch'nguñ**	ឆ្ងាញ់
delighted	**dtrayk-or**	ត្រេកអរ
depart	**jeuñ**	ចេញ
dessert	**bong-aim**	បង្អែម
diamond	**bpeutch**	ពេជ្រ
diarrhoea	**roak joh ree-uk**	រោគចុះរាក
dictionary	**wuch-a-na-nOO-grom**	វចនានុក្រម
die	**s'lup**	ស្លាប់
different	**koh; bplaik**	ខុស; ប្លែក
difficult	**bpi-baak; lOOm-baak**	ពិបាក; លំបាក
diplomat	**dtoot**	ទូត
direct (adj)	**dtrong**	ត្រង់
dirty	**gror-kwok**	ក្រខ្វក់
disabled	**bpi-gaa**	ពិការ
disappear	**but**	បាត់
disease	**roak; jOOm-ngeu**	រោគ; ជម្ងឺ
dish	**jaan**	ចាន
distance	**jom-ngai**	ចម្ងាយ

district	s'rok	ស្រុក
do	t'wer	ធ្វើ
doctor	bpairt; kroo bpairt	ពេទ្យ; គ្រូពេទ្យ
dog	ch'kai	ឆ្កែ
dollar	dol-laa	ដុល្លា
don't	gom . . . (ay)	កុំ . . . (ទេ)
door	twee-a	ទ្វារ
downstairs	joa-un graom	ជាន់ក្រោម
dress (n)	som-lee-uk bom-bpay-uk	សម្លៀកបំពាក់
dress (v)	s'lee-uk bpay-uk	ស្លៀកពាក់
drink (v)	peuk	ផឹក
drive (a vehicle)	bark (laan)	បើក(ឡាន)
driver	nay-uk bark laan	អ្នកបើកឡាន
drug (medicine)	t'num	ថ្នាំ
drunk	s'ra-weung	ស្រវឹង
dry	s'ngoo-ut	ស្ងួត
duck	dtee-a	ទា
during	ra-wee-ung	រវាង
duty	ngee-a	ងារ
dysentery	(jOOm-ngeu) moo-ul	(ជម្ងឺ)មូល
each	ni-moo-ay	និមួយ
early (morning)	bpreuk	ព្រឹក
earn a living	rork see	រកស៊ី
east	kaang gart	ខាងកើត
easy	s'roo-ul	ស្រួល
eat	bpi-saa (*polite*);	ពិសា
	n'yum (*colloq.*)	ញ៉ាំ
education	gaa seuk-saa	ការសិក្សា

egg	**bporng**	ពង
electricity	**uk-gee-sa-nee**	អគ្គីសនី
embassy	**s'taan dtoot**	ស្ថានទូត
empty	**dtor-dtay; dtOOm-nay**	ទទេ; ទំនេ
end	**jong**	ចុង
engine	**kreu-ung yoo-un**	គ្រឿងយន្ត
engineer	**wi-s'waa-gor**	វិស្វករ
English	**ong-klayh**	អង់គ្លេស
enjoy	**sop-bai**	សប្បាយ
enough	**l'morm**	ល្មម
enter	**joal**	ចូល
envelope	**s'raom som-bot**	ស្រោមសំបុត្រ
era	**sa-mai**	សម័យ
evening	**l'ngee-uch**	ល្ងាច
event, situation	**hait-gaa**	ហេតុការណ៍
ever: to have ever done something	**dail**	ដែល
every	**roa-ul**	រាល់
exam: take an exam	**bra-lorng**	ប្រឡង
example	**gOOm-roo; dtoo-a yaang**	គំរូ; តួយ៉ាង
excuse (v)	**soam dtoah**	សូមទោស
excuse me	**soam dtoah**	សូមទោស
expensive	**t'lai**	ថ្លៃ
extremely	**bpayk**	ពេក
eye	**p'nairk**	ភ្នែក
face (n)	**mOOk**	មុខ
factory	**roang juk**	រោងចក្រ

family	kroo-a-saa	គ្រួសារ
famine	gaa ot bai	ការ អត់បាយ
famous	l'bay	ល្បី
fan (n) (electric)	dong-hul	ដង្ហាល់
far	ch'ngai	ឆ្ងាយ
fare	t'lai ch'noo-ul	ថ្លៃឈ្នួល
farmer	nay-uk s'rai	អ្នកស្រែ
fast	chup	ឆាប់
fat (adj)	dtoa-ut	ធាត់
father	oa-bpOOk	ឪពុក
fear (v)	k'laich	ខ្លាច
fence	ra-borng	របង
fever	jOOm-ngeu grOOn g'dao	ជម្ងឺគ្រុនក្ដៅ
few	dteuch	តិច
film (movie)	gon	កុន
(for camera)	feem tort roop	ហ្វីមថតរូប
find	rork kerñ	រកឃើញ
finished	jop	ចប់
fire (n)	plerng cheh	ភ្លើងឆេះ
first	dtee moo-ay	ទីមួយ
fish (n)	dt'ray	ត្រី
fix (v) (repair)	joo-ah jOOl	ជួសជុល
fix (v) (e.g. price)	gom-not	កំណត់
flat (adj)	ree-up s'mar	រៀបស្មើ
flat (n)	p'dtay-ah l'wairng	ផ្ទះល្វែង
flower (n)	p'gaa	ផ្កា
food (rice)	bai; m'hoap	បាយ;ម្ហូប
foot	jerng	ជើង

for	**som-rup**	សម្រាប់
forbid	**haam**	ហាម
force (v)	**bong-kom**	បង្ខំ
foreign	**bor-ra-dtayh**	បរទេស
foreigner	**joo-un bor-ra-dtayh**	ជនបរទេស
forest	**bpray-ee**	ព្រៃ
forget	**pleuch**	ភ្លេច
free (no charge)	**ot bong t'lai**	ឥតបង់ថ្លៃ
free time	**dtOOm-nay**	ទំនេរ
French	**baa-rung**	បារាំង
friend	**bpoo-uk maak; meut**	ពួកម៉ាក; មិត្ត
Friday	**t'ngai sok**	ថ្ងៃសុក្រ
from	**bpee**	ពី
front	**mOOk**	មុខ
fruit	**plai cher**	ផ្លែឈើ
full	**bpeuñ**	ពេញ
(from eating)	**cha-ait**	ឆ្អែត
funny	**gom-bplaing**	កំប្លែង
game	**l'baing**	ល្បែង
garden	**soo-un**	សួន
gate	**t'wee-a**	ទ្វារ
gem	**t'boang**	ត្បូង
general: in general	**jee-a dtoo dtou**	ជាទូទៅ
German	**aa-leu-mong**	អាឡឺម៉ង់
get	**baan**	បាន
gift	**jOOm-noon**	ជំនូន
girl	**k'mayng s'ray**	ក្មេងស្រី

give	ao-ee	ឱ្យ (អោយ)
glass (n)	gai-o	កែវ
glasses (spectacles)	wain dtaa	វ៉ែនតា
glue	gao	កាវ
go	dtou	ទៅ
gold	mee-ah	មាស
good	la-or	ល្អ
goodbye	lee-a seun hai-ee	លាសិនហើយ
grade	t'nuk	ថ្នាក់
graduate (v)	ree-un jop	រៀនចប់
grandchild	jao	ចៅ
granddaughter	jao s'ray	ចៅស្រី
grandfather	jee-dtaa; dtaa	ជីតា; តា
grandmother	jee doan; yee-ay	ជីដូន; យាយ
grandson	jao bproh	ចៅប្រុស
grass	s'mao	ស្មៅ
green	bpoa-a bai dtorng	ពណ៌បៃតង
greet	jOOm-ree-up soo-a	ជំរាបសួរ
ground	day	ដី
group	bpoo-uk; grom	ពួក; ក្រុម
grow (plants)	dum	ដាំ
guarantee (v)	rup-rorng	រ៉ាប់រង
guest	p'nyee-o	ភ្ញៀវ
gun	gum-plerng	កាំភ្លើង

hair	sok	សក់
half	gon-lah	កន្លះ
hand	day	ដៃ

happen	**gart; gart larng**	កើត; កើតឡើង
happy	**sop-bai**	សប្បាយ
harbour	**pai**	ផៃ
hardly	**meun sou ...**	មិនសូវ ...
hat	**moo-uk**	មួក
hate (v)	**sa-op**	ស្អប់
have	**mee-un**	មាន
have to, must	**dtrou**	ត្រូវ
he	**goa-ut**	គាត់
head (of body)	**g'baal**	ក្បាល
headache	**cheu g'baal**	ឈឺក្បាល
health	**sok-ka-pee-up**	សុខភាព
hear	**leu**	ឮ
heart	**jeut**	ចិត្ត
heavy	**t'ngoo-un**	ធ្ងន់
help (v)	**joo-ay**	ជួយ
here	**ai nih**	ឯនេះ
high	**k'bpoo-ah**	ខ្ពស់
hill	**p'nOOm**	ភ្នំ
hire	**joo-ul**	ជួល
hit (v)	**wee-ay**	វាយ
hold	**gun**	កាន់
holiday	**t'ngai chOOp som-raak**	ថ្ងៃឈប់សម្រាក
home	**p'dtay-ah**	ផ្ទះ
homesick	**neuk p'dtay-ah**	នឹកផ្ទះ
honest	**dtee-ung dtrong**	ទៀងត្រង់
hope (v)	**song-keum**	សង្ឃឹម
hospital	**mOOn-dtee bpairt**	មន្ទីរពេទ្យ

hot	**g'dao**	ក្តៅ
(spicy)	**heul; har**	ហឹល; ហើរ
hotel	**son-ta-gee-a**	សណ្ឋាគារ
hour	**maong**	ម៉ោង
house	**p'dtay-ah**	ផ្ទះ
how?	**yaang maych?**	យ៉ាងម៉េច
how many?	**bpon-maan?**	ប៉ុន្មាន
human (n)	**ma-nOOh**	មនុស្ស
hungry	**klee-un**	ឃ្លាន
hurry	**bpra-n'yup**	ប្រញ៉ាប់
husband	**b'day**	ប្ដី
I	**k'nyom**	ខ្ញុំ
ice	**dteuk gork**	ទឹកកក
idea	**gom-neut**	គំនិត
if	**bar**	បើ
ill	**cheu**	ឈឺ
illness	**jOOm-ngeu**	ជម្ងឺ
immediately	**plee-um**	ភ្លាម
impolite	**ot goo-a som**	ឥតគួរសម
important	**som-kun**	សំខាន់
in	**k'nong**	ក្នុង
industry	**OO-saa-ha-gum**	ឧស្សាហកម្ម
inspect	**dtroo-ut**	ត្រួត
intelligent	**mee-un bpraach-nyaa**	មានប្រាជ្ញា
intend	**geut**	គិត
interested	**jup jeut**	ចាប់ចិត្ត
interpreter	**nay-uk bork bprai**	អ្នកបកប្រែ

invite (v)	**uñ-jerñ**	អញ្ជើញ
is	**jee-a; geu**	ជា; គឺ
Islam	**eu-s'laam**	អ៊ិស្លាម
it	**wee-a**	វា
Japanese	**jee-bpOOn**	ជប៉ុន; ជប៉ុន
job	**gaa**	ការ
join (v)	**roo-um**	រួម
juice: fruit juice	**dteuk plai cher**	ទឹកផ្លែឈើ
jump	**loat**	លោត
jungle	**bprau-ee**	ព្រៃ
just (fair)	**dtreum dtrou**	ត្រឹមត្រូវ
just: I have just . . .	**k'nyom dterp dtai . . .**	ខ្ញុំទើបតែ . . .
justice	**yOOt-dta-toa-a**	យុត្តិធម៌
key	**goan sao**	កូនសោ
Khmer	**k'mai**	ខ្មែរ
kill	**som-lup**	សម្លាប់
kilogram	**gee-loa-graam**	គីឡូក្រាម
kilometre	**gee-loa-mait**	គីឡូម៉ែត្រ
kind (adj)	**jeut la-or**	ចិត្តល្អ
kind (n)	**yaang; baip**	យ៉ាង; បែប
knife	**gum-beut**	កាំបិត
know (a person)	**s'koa-ul**	ស្គាល់
(information)	**deung**	ដឹង
(how to do something)	**jeh**	ចេះ

label	s'laak	ស្លាក
lack (v)	kwah	ខ្វះ
lake	beung	បឹង
lamp (electric)	jong-gee-ung	ចង្កៀង
land (n) (ground, soil)	day	ដី
landlord	m'jah p'dtay-ah	ម្ចាស់ផ្ទះ
language	pee-a-saa	ភាសា
large	tom	ធំ
last: last week	aa-dteut mOOn	អាទិត្យមុន
late	yeut	យឺត
later, subsequently	grao-ee moak	ក្រោយមក
lazy	k'jeul	ខ្ជិល
learn	ree-un	រៀន
leave (depart)	jaak-jeuñ	ចាកចេញ
left (side)	ch'wayng	ឆ្វេង
leg	jerng	ជើង
let (v) (allow)	ao-ee	ឱ្យ; អោយ
letter (post)	som-bot	សំបុត្រ
letter (alphabet)	dtoo-a ok-sor	តួអក្សរ
library	bun-naa-lai	បណ្ណល័យ
licence (driving)	som-bot bark-bor roat-ta-yOOn	សំបុត្របើកបរ រថយន្ត
lie (v) (down)	dtOOm-rayt	ទំរេត
lie (v) (tell a lie)	go-hok	កុហក
life	jee-weut	ជីវិត
like (want, enjoy)	jong; joal jeut	ចង់; ចូលចិត្ត
like (similar)	doach	ដូច
liquor	s'raa	ស្រា

listen	s'dup	ស្តាប់
litre	leet	លីត្រ
little	dtoach	តូច
live (v)	nou	នៅ
lock (v)	juk sao	ចាក់សោ
long (size)	wairng	វែង
(time)	yoo	យូរ
look (at)	merl	មើល
look (for)	rork merl	រកមើល
look out!	bpra-yut	ប្រយ័ត្ន
lose (something)	but	បាត់
loud	klung	ខ្លាំង
love (v)	s'ra-luñ	ស្រឡាញ់
lovely	la-or	ល្អ
lower (v) (the price)	boñ-joh (dtom-lai)	បញ្ចុះ(តម្លៃ)
luck	som-naang	សំណាង
lunch	bai t'ngai dtrong	បាយថ្ងៃត្រង់
machine	maa-seen	ម៉ាស៊ីន
mad (crazy, insane)	ch'goo-ut	ឆ្កួត
(angry)	keung	ខឹង
make	t'wer	ធ្វើ
malaria	jOOm-ngeu grOOn juñ	ជម្ងឺគ្រុនចាញ់
many	j'rarn	ច្រើន
map	pain-dtee	ផែនទី
market	p'saa	ផ្សារ
married	gaa hai-ee	ការហើយ
match	cher-gooh	ឈើគូស

meat	sai-ich	សាច់
medicine	t'num bpairt	ថ្នាំពេទ្យ
meet	joo-up	ជួប
metre	mait	ម៉ែត្រ
middle	gon-daal	កណ្ដាល
might, may	aach ... baan	អាច ... បាន
mine (n) (explosive)	kroa-up meen	គ្រាប់មីន
minute	nee-a-dtee	នាទី
mirror	goñ-jok	កញ្ចក់
mistake	gom-hoh	កំហុស
moment	plairt	ភ្លែត
Monday	t'ngai jun	ថ្ងៃចន្ទ
money	bpruk; loo-ee	ប្រាក់; លុយ
month	kai	ខែ
more	dtee-ut	ទៀត
morning	bpreuk	ព្រឹក
mosquito	mooh	មូស
most (the majority)	pee-uk j'rarn	ភាគច្រើន
most (superlative)	j'rarn jee-ung gay	ច្រើនជាងគេ
mother	m'dai	ម្ដាយ
motorcycle	moa-dtoa	ម៉ូតូ
mountain	p'nOOm	ភ្នំ
mouse, rat	gon-dol	កណ្ដុរ
move (house)	plah p'dtay-ah	ផ្លាស់ផ្ទះ
much	j'rarn	ច្រើន
museum	saa-ra-mOOn-dtee	សារមន្ទីរ
music	playng; don-dtray	ភ្លេង; ដន្ត្រី
must	dtrou	ត្រូវ

name (n)	ch'moo-ah	ឈ្មោះ
namely	geu	គឺ
narcotics	kreu-ung ñee-un	គ្រឿងញៀន
narrow	jong-ee-ut	ចង្អៀត
nation	jee-ut	ជាតិ
nationality	joo-un-jee-ut	ជនជាតិ
nature (natural world)	toa-um-ma-jee-ut	ធម្មជាតិ
near	jeut	ជិត
nearly	ster tai	ស្ទើតៃ
neat, tidy	sa-aat baat	ស្អាតបាត
necessary	jum-baich	ចាំបាច់
need (v)	dtrou-gaa	ត្រូវការ
net (mosquito)	mOOng	មុង
never	meun dail ...	មិនដែល ...
never mind	meun ay dtay	មិនអ្វីទេ
new	t'may	ថ្មី
newspaper	gaa-sait	កាសែត
next	bon-dtoa-up	បន្ទាប់
next month	kai grao-ee	ខែក្រោយ
nice	la-or	ល្អ
night	yOOp	យប់
no	dtay	ទេ
noodles	goo-ee dtee-o	គុយទាវ
normal	toa-um-ma-daa	ធម្មតា
north	kaang jerng	ខាងជើង
notice (n)	bpra-gaah	ប្រកាស
notice (v)	song-gayt	សង្កេត
now	ay-lou nih	ពេលនេះ

nowadays	sop t'ngai nih	សព្វថ្ងៃនេះ
number (quantity)	jom-noo-un	ចំនួន
(figure)	layk	លេខ
observe	song-gayt	សង្កេត
occur	gart larng	កើតឡើង
of	ra-boh	របស់
office	ga-ri-yaa-lai	ការិយាល័យ
often	ñeuk ñoa-up	ញឹកញាប់
oil (n)	bprayng	ប្រេង
old (things, people)	jah	ចាស់
on	nou ler	នៅលើ
once (one time)	m'dorng	ម្ដង
oneself	kloo-un aing	ខ្លួនឯង
only	dtai ... bon-noh;	តែ ... ប៉ុណ្ណោះ ;
	groa-un dtai	គ្រាន់តែ
open	bark	បើក
opportunity	oa-gaah	ឱកាស
or	reu	ឬ
ordinary	toa-um-ma-daa	ធម្មតា
organisation	ong-gaa	អង្គារ
other	ai dtee-ut	ឯទៀត
ought	goo-a dtai	គួរតែ
outside	kaang grao	ខាងក្រៅ
over (above)	ler	លើ
owner	m'jah	ម្ចាស់
package	goñ-jop	កញ្ចប់

paddy field	s'rai	ស្រែ
pain	cheu	ឈឺ
painting (picture)	gOOm-noo	គំនូរ
pair	goo	គូ
paper	gra-daah	ក្រដាស
parents	oa-bpOOk m'dai	ឪពុកម្ដាយ
park (n)	soo-un	សួន
park (v) (a car)	jort (laan)	ចត (ឡាន)
part	pee-uk; p'naik; jom-naik	ភាគ; ផ្នែក; ចំណែក
passenger	nay-uk dom-nar	អ្នកដំណើរ
patient (n)	nay-uk jOOm-ngeu	អ្នកជម្ងឺ
pay (v)	bong t'lai	បង់ថ្លៃ
peace	son-dti-pee-up	សន្តិភាព
pen (for writing)	bpaa-gaa	ប៉ាកា
pencil	k'mao dai	ខ្មៅដៃ
people	bpra-jee-a-joo-un	ប្រជាជន
perhaps	bpra-hail	ប្រហែល
person	ma-nOOh	មនុស្ស
petrol	bprayng sung	ប្រេងសាំង
Phnom Penh	p'nOOm bpeuñ	ភ្នំពេញ
photocopy (v)	tort aik-ga-saa	ថតឯកសារ
photograph (n)	roop tort	រូបថត
photograph (v)	tort roop	ថតរូប
piece	dom	ដុំ
pig	ch'rook	ជ្រូក
pill, tablet	t'num kroa-up; t'num layp	ថ្នាំគ្រាប់; ថ្នាំលេប
place (n)	gon-laing	កន្លែង
plate	jaan	ចាន

play (v)	**layng**	លេង
police, policeman	**dtom-roo-ut**	តម្រួត
polite	**goo-a sorm**	គួរសម
politician	**nay-uk nee-yoa-bai**	អ្នកនយោបាយ
politics, policy	**nee-yoa-bai**	នយោបាយ
poor	**gror**	ក្រ
population	**bpra-jee-joo-un**	ប្រជាជន
pork	**sai-ich ch'rook**	សាច់ជ្រូក
port	**pai**	ផៃ
postcard	**bprai-sa-nee-ya-bot**	ប្រៃសណីយបត្រ
post-office	**bprai-sa-nee-ya-taan**	ប្រៃសណីយដ្ឋាន
pot (cooking)	**ch'nung**	ឆ្នាំង
powder	**m'sao**	ម្សៅ
power (influence)	**om-nai-ich**	អំណាច
practise	**hut**	ហាត់
pregnant	**mee-un p'dteu-ee bpoo-ah**	មានផ្ទៃពោះ
prepare	**bom-rong; ree-up jom**	បំរុង; រៀបចំ
pretty	**la-or; la-or sa-aat**	ល្អ; ល្អស្អាត
previous	**mOOn**	មុន
price	**dtom-lai; t'lai**	តម្លៃ; ថ្លៃ
prison	**gOOk**	គុក
probably	**mOOk jee-a**	មុខជា
problem	**bpuñ-ña-haa**	បញ្ហា
profit	**gom-rai**	កំរៃ
progress (v)	**jom-rarn**	ចំរើន
prohibit	**haam**	ហាម
promise (v)	**son-yaa**	សន្យា
province	**kait**	ខេត្រ

put	**duk**	ដាក់
quality	**kOOn-na-pee-up**	គុណភាព
quantity	**jom-noo-un**	ចំនួន
queer, unusual	**bplaik**	ខ្ពែក
question (n)	**som-noo-a**	សំនួរ
quick	**chup**	ឆាប់
quiet	**s'ngut**	ស្ងាត់
radio	**wit-yOO**	វិទ្យុ
rain (n, v)	**plee-ung**	ភ្លៀង
rate	**ut-dtraa**	អត្រា
reach (arrive)	**dol**	ដល់
read	**merl; aan**	មើល; អាន
ready	**ree-up jum hai**	រៀបចំហើយ
real (true)	**bpeut; mairn dtairn**	ពិត; មែនទែន
reason	**hait**	ហេតុ
receipt	**bong-gun dai**	បង្កាន់ដៃ
receive	**dtor-dtoo-ul**	ទទួល
recently	**t'may t'may nih**	ថ្មី ៗ នេះ
red	**bpoa-a gra-horm**	ពណ៌ក្រហម
refrigerator	**dtoo dteuk kork**	ទូទឹកកក
refugee	**joo-un pee-ah kloo-un**	ជនភៀសខ្លួន
refugee camp	**jOOm-rOOm joo-un pee-ah kloo-un**	ជំរំជនភៀសខ្លួន
refuse (v)	**meun bprorm**	មិនព្រម
relative (kin)	**nyee-ut son-daan**	ញាតិសន្តាន
religion	**saa-s'naa**	សាសនា

remember	**jum**	ចាំ
rent (n)	**ch'noo-ul**	ឈ្នួល
rent (v)	**joo-ul**	ជួល
repair (v)	**joo-ah jol**	ជួសជុល
request (v)	**som; soam**	សំ; សូម
reserve, book	**bom-rong dtOOk**	បំរុងទុក
respect (v)	**goa-rOOp**	គោរព
rest (v)	**som-raak**	សំម្រាក
restaurant	**haang bai;**	ហាងបាយ;
	poa-ja-nee-ya-taan	ភោជនីយដ្ឋាន
return	**dtra-lop**	ត្រឡប់
rice (cooked)	**bai**	បាយ
rich, wealthy	**mee-un**	មាន
right (opposite of left)	**s'dum**	ស្ដាំ
(correct)	**dtrou**	ត្រូវ
river	**dtoo-un-lay**	ទន្លេ
road	**plou; t'nol**	ផ្លូវ; ថ្នល់
rob	**bplon**	ប្លន់
robber	**jao**	ចោរ
room	**bon-dtOOp**	បន្ទប់
rope	**k'sai**	ខ្សែ
run	**roo-ut**	រត់
Russia	**rOO-see**	រុស្សី
sad	**bproo-ay; bproo-ay jeut**	ព្រួយ; ព្រួយចិត្ត
safe	**k'mee-un kroo-ah t'nuk**	គ្មានគ្រោះថ្នាក់
salary	**bpruk kai**	ប្រាក់ខែ
salt	**om-beul**	អំបិល

same	**dor-dail**	ដដែល
satisfied	**bpeuñ jeut**	ពេញចិត្ត
Saturday	**t'ngai sao**	ថ្ងៃសៅរ៍
say	**ni-yee-ay taa**	និយាយថា
scared	**klai-ich**	ខ្លាច
scarf	**gror-maa**	ក្រមា
school	**saa-laa ree-un**	សាលារៀន
science	**wit-yee-a-saah**	វិទ្យាសាស្ត្រ
scissors	**gon-dtrai**	កន្ត្រៃ
scream	**s'raik**	ស្រែក
sea	**sa-mot**	សមុទ្រ
season	**ra-dou**	រដូវ
hot season	**ra-dou g'dao**	រដូវក្ដៅ
rainy season	**ra-dou plee-ung**	រដូវភ្លៀង
cool season	**ra-dou ra-ngee-a**	រដូវរងា
second (unit of time)	**wi-nee-a-dtee**	វិនាទី
secret (adj)	**som-ngut**	សម្ងាត់
secretary	**lay-kaa-ti-gaa**	លេខាធិការ
section	**pee-uk; p'naik**	ភាគ; ផ្នែក
see	**kerñ**	ឃើញ
self	**kloo-un aing**	ខ្លួនឯង
selfish	**geut dtai kloo-un aing**	គិតតែខ្លួនឯង
sell	**loo-uk**	លក់
send	**p'nyar**	ផ្ញើរ
servant	**nay-uk bom-rar**	អ្នកបំរើ
serve	**bom-rar**	បំរើ
set (n) (of items)	**chOOt; som-rup**	ឈុត; សម្រាប់
several	**bay boo-un**	បីប៉ុន

sew	day	ដេរ
shampoo (n)	t'num gok	ថ្នាំកក់
shape	roop ree-ung	រូបរាង
shave	gao bpOOk moa-ut	ការពុកមាត់
ship (n)	g'bul	កប៉ាល់
shirt	ao	អាវ
shoe(s)	s'baik jerng	ស្បែកជើង
shoot (v)	buñ	បាញ់
shop (n)	haang	ហាង
short	klay	ខ្លី
shout (v)	s'raik	ស្រែក
show (v)	bong-haañ	បង្ហាញ
shower (v)	ngoot dteuk	ងូតទឹក
shut	bpeut	បិទ
shy	ee-un	អៀន
sick	cheu; meun sroo-ul kloo-un	ឈឺ; មិនស្រួលខ្លួន
side	kaang	ខាង
silent	s'ngee-um	ស្ងៀម
silver	bpruk	ប្រាក់
similar	bpra-hail k'nee-a	ប្រហែលគ្នា
since	dtung bpee	តាំងពី
sing	ch'ree-ung	ច្រៀង
sister: older sister	borng s'ray	បងស្រី
younger sister	bpa-oan s'ray	ប្អូនស្រី
sit	ong-goo-ee	អង្គុយ
situated	nou	នៅ
situation, state of affairs	s'taan-na-gaa	ស្ថានការណ៍

size	dtOOm-hOOm	ទំហំ
skilled	beun bpra-sop; bpoo-gai	ពិនប្រសប់; ពូកែ
skin	s'baik	ស្បែក
skirt	som-bpoo-ut	សំពត់
sky	mayk	មេឃ
sleep (v)	dayk; som-raan	ដេក; សម្រាន្ត
sleepy	ngor-ngoo-ee dayk	ងងុយដេក
slow	yeut	យឺត
small	dtoa-ich	តូច
smell (n)	gleun	ក្លិន
smile (v)	nyor-nyeum	ញញឹម
smoke (v) (cigarette)	jork (baa-ray)	ជក់(បារី)
smooth	ree-up	រាប
snake	bporh	ពស់
so	doach-neh	ដូច្នេះ
so that	darm-bay	ដើម្បី
soap	saa-boo	សាប៊ូ
society	song-gOOm	សង្គម
sock(s)	s'raom jerng	ស្រោមជើង
soldier	dtee-a-hee-un	ទាហាន
some	klah	ខ្លះ
son	goan bproh	កូនប្រុស
song	jom-ree-ung	ចម្រៀង
soon	nou bpayl jeut jeut nih	នៅពេលជិត ៗ នេះ
sorry (regret)	s'dai	ស្តាយ
sorry (apologize)	soam dtoah	សូមទោស
sour	joo	ជូរ
south	kaang t'boang	ខាងត្បូង

speak	ni-yee-ay	និយាយ
special	bpi-sayh	ពិសេស
spend	jom-nai; brar; jai	ចំណាយ; ប្រើ; ចាយ
spicy (food)	heul	ហឹរ
spoon	s'laap bpree-a	ស្លាបព្រា
sport	gay-laa	កីឡា
stairs	gum jOOn-dar	កាំជណ្ដើរ
stamp (n)	dtaim	តែមប្រិ៍
stand (v)	chor	ឈរ
start, begin	jup p'darm	ចាប់ផ្ដើម
starve, be starving	ot bai; ot klee-un	អត់បាយ; អត់ឃ្លាន
station	s'taa-nee	ស្ថានីយ
stay (at hotel)	s'nuk nou; som-raak	ស្នាក់នៅ; សម្រាក
steal	loo-uch	លួច
still (adv)	nou . . . nou lar-ee	នៅ . . . នៅឡើយ
stingy, mean	gom-nuñ	កំណាញ់
stomach	bpoo-ah	ពោះ
stone	t'mor	ថ្ម
stop (v)	chOOp	ឈប់
store, shop	haang	ហាង
story	reu-ung	រឿង
straight	dtrong	ត្រង់
strange	bplaik; jom-laik	ប្លែក; ចំឡែក
street	wi-tay; plou	វិថី; ផ្លូវ
strength	gom-lung	កម្លាំង
strike (v), hit	wee-ay	វាយ
string	k'sai	ខ្សែ
strong	klung	ខ្លាំង

student	**goan seuh; ni-seut**	កូនសិស្ស; និស្សិត
study (v)	**ree-un**	រៀន
stupid	**klao**	ខ្លៅ
such as	**doach jee-a**	ដូចជា
suddenly	**s'rup dtai**	ស្រាប់តែ
sugar	**s'gor**	ស្ករ
suitable	**som-rOOm**	សមរម្យ
sun	**ah-dteut**	អាទិត្យ
Sunday	**t'ngai ah-dteut**	ថ្ងៃអាទិត្យ
suppose	**s'maan**	ស្មាន
supposed to	**dtrou dtai**	ត្រូវតែ
sure: for sure	**jee-a bpraa-got**	ជាប្រាកដ
surprised	**p'nyay-uk**	ភ្ញាក់
sweat (v)	**baik nyerh**	បែកញើស
sweep	**baoh**	ច្រោស
sweet (taste)	**pa-aim**	ផ្អែម
swim	**hail dteuk**	ហែលទឹក
system	**ra-borp; ra-bee-up**	របប; របៀប
table	**dtoh**	តុ
take	**yoak**	យក
talk (v)	**ni-yee-ay**	និយាយ
tall	**k'bpoo-ah**	ខ្ពស់
tasty	**ch'nguñ**	ឆ្ងាញ់
taxi	**dtuk-see**	តាក់ស៊ី
tea	**dtai; dteuk dtai**	តែ; ទឹកតែ
teach	**bong-ree-un**	បង្រៀន
teacher	**kroo bong-ree-un**	គ្រូបង្រៀន

telegram	**dtoo-ra-layk**	ទូរលេខ
telephone (n, v)	**dtoo-ra-sup**	ទូរស័ព្
television	**dtoo-ra-dtoa-a**	ទូរទស្សន៍
tell	**bprup**	ប្រាប់
temple	**woa-ut**	វត្ត
Thai	**tai**	ថៃ
than	**jee-ung**	ជាង
thank, thank you	**or-gOOn**	អរគុណ
that	**nOOh**	នោះ
theatre	**roang l'kaon**	រោងល្ខោន
then (at that time)	**bpayl nOOh**	ពេលនោះ
then (after that)	**roo-ich**	រួច
there	**ai nOOh**	ឯនោះ
therefore	**uñ-jeung**	អញ្ចឹង
they	**gay**	គេ
thick	**grah**	ក្រាស់
thief	**jao**	ចោរ
thin (things)	**s'darng**	ស្តើង
thin (people)	**s'gorm**	ស្គម
thing(s)	**ra-boh**	របស់
think	**geut; yoo-ul**	គិត; យល់
thirsty	**s'rayk dteuk**	ស្រេកទឹក
this	**nih**	នេះ
thousand	**bpoa-un**	ពាន់
ten thousand	**meun**	ម៉ឺន
hundred thousand	**sain**	សែន
throw (v)	**boh; gra-wut; jaol**	ប្រោះ; ក្រវាត់; ចោល
Thursday	**t'ngai bpra-hoa-ah**	ថ្ងៃព្រហស្បតិ៍

ticket	som-bot	សំបុត្រ
tidy	ree-up roy; sa-aat baat	រៀបរយ; ស្អាតប្អាត
tie (v)	jong; jong p'joap	ចង; ចងភ្ជាប់
tie, necktie	gra-wut	ក្រវ៉ាត់
tight (clothes)	teung	តឹង
time	bpayl; way-lee-a; gaal	ពេល; វេលា; កាល
tired (exhausted)	neu-ay hot	នឿយហត់
tired of, bored	neu-ay nai;	នឿយណាយ;
	tOOñ dtroa-un	ធុញទ្រាន់
to, towards	dol	ដល់
to, in order to	darm-bay	ដើម្បី
tobacco	t'num jork	ថ្នាំជក់
today	t'ngai nih	ថ្ងៃនេះ
together	ji-moo-ay k'nee-a	ជាមួយគ្នា
toilet	bong-goo-un	បង្គន់
tomorrow	sa-aik	ស្អែក
tonight	yOOp nih	យប់នេះ
too, also	dai; porng	ដែរ; ផង
too . . . (too much)	. . . j'rarn bpayk	. . . ច្រើនពេក
tooth	t'mayñ	ធ្មេញ
toothbrush	j'raah doh t'mayñ	ច្រាសដុសធ្មេញ
toothpaste	m'sao doh t'mayñ	ម្សៅដុសធ្មេញ
toothpick	cher juk t'mayñ	ឈើចាក់ធ្មេញ
top, on top	kaang ler	ខាងលើ
touch (v)	bpah; bpoa-ul	ប៉ះ; ពាល់
tourist	nay-uk dtay-sa-jor	អ្នកទេសចរណ៍
towel	gon-saing	កន្សែង
town	dtee grong; p'saa	ទីក្រុង; ផ្សារ

trade (v)	jOOm-noo-uñ	ជំនួញ
traffic	ja-raa-jor	ចរាចរ
train (n)	ror-dtayh plerng	រទេះភ្លើង
translate	bork-bprai	បកប្រែ
translator	nay-uk bork bprai	អ្នកបកប្រែ
travel (v)	t'wer dom-nar	ធ្វើដំណើរ
tray	taah	ថាស
tree	darm cher	ដើមឈើ
trousers	kao	ខោ
true	bpeut; bpeut mairn	ពិត; ពិតមែន
trust (v)	(jeu-a) dtOOk jeut	(ជឿ)ទុកចិត្ត
try out,try on	lor merl	លមើល
try, persevere	kom bp'yee-a yee-um	ខំព្យាយាម
turn (left or right)	bot	បត់
turn on (a switch)	bark	បើក
turn off (a switch)	beut	បិទ
type (n)	baip	បែប
type (v)	wee-ay duk-dtee-loa	វាយដាក់ទីឡ
typewriter	duk-dtee-loa; maa-seen	ដាក់ទីឡ;
	ong-goo-lee layk	ម៉ាស៊ីនអង្គុលីលេខ
ugly	aa-grok merl	អាក្រក់មើល
umbrella	chut	ឆ័ត្រ
under	graom; kaang graom	ក្រោម; ខាងក្រោម
understand	yoo-ul	យល់
unhappy	meun sa-bai	មិនសប្បាយ
United States	sa-haa roa-ut aa-may-rik	សហរដ្ឋអាមេរិក
university	saa-gol wit-yee-a-lai	សាកលវិទ្យាល័យ

up: get up, go up	**larng**	ឡើង
upstairs	**joa-un ler**	ជាន់លើ
urgent	**bon-dtoa-un**	បន្ទាន់
us	**yerng**	យើង
use (v)	**brar**	ប្រើ
used to, accustomed to	**t'loa-up nęung**	ធ្លាប់នឹង
used to, formerly . . .	**t'loa-up**	ធ្លាប់
useful	**mee-un bpra-yaoch**	មានប្រយោជន៍
useless	**k'mee-un bpra-yaoch**	គ្មានប្រយោជន៍
usually	**toa-um-ma-daa**	ធម្មតា
vacant	**dtOOm-nay**	ទំនេរ
vacation	**wi-sa-ma-gaal**	វិស្សមកាល
value	**dtom-lai**	តម្លៃ
various	**p'sayng p'sayng**	ផ្សេង ៗ
vase	**toa**	ថូ
vegetable	**bon-lai**	បន្លែ
vendor	**nay-uk loo-uk**	អ្នកលក់
very	**nah**	ណាស់
not very . . .	**meun sou . . .**	មិនសូវ . . .
Vietnam	**wee-ut naam**	វៀតណាម
view (scenic view)	**dtay-sa-pee-up**	ទេសភាព
village	**poom**	ភូមិ
villager	**nay-uk poom**	អ្នកភូមិ
visit (v)	**dtou layng**	ទៅលេង
visitor, guest	**p'nyee-o**	ភ្ញៀវ
voice	**som-layng**	សម្លេង

wait	jum	ចាំ
wake up, awaken	p'nyay-uk	ភ្ញាក់
walk	dar	ដើរ
wallet	gah-boap bpruk	កាបូបប្រាក់
want	jong	ចង់
war	jom-bung; song-kree-um	ចំបាំង; សង្គ្រាម
wardrobe	dtoo kao-ao	ទូខោអាវ
warm	g'dao	ក្តៅ
wash	doh lee-ung	ដុសលាង
waste (v)	k'jay-ah k'jee-ay	ខ្ជះខ្ជាយ
watch (n)	nee-a-li-gaa dai	នាឡិកាដៃ
watch (v)	merl	មើល
watch out!	bpra-yut	ប្រយ័ត្ន
water (n)	dteuk	ទឹក
way (route, path)	plou	ផ្លូវ
way (method, means)	wi-tee; ra-bee-up	វិធី; របៀប
we	yerng	យើង
weak	k'sao-ee	ខ្សោយ
wealthy	mee-un	មាន
weapon	aa-wOOt	អាវុធ
wear (clothes)	slee-uk bpay-uk	ស្លៀកពាក់
(upper garment)	bpay-uk	ពាក់
(lower garment)	slee-uk	ស្លៀក
wed, marry	ree-up gaa	រៀបការ
Wednesday	t'ngai bpOOt	ថ្ងៃពុធ
week	aa-dteut	អាទិត្យ
weight	dtOOm-ngoo-un	ទម្ងន់
well (healthy)	sok-sop-bai	សុខសប្បាយ

west	kaang laych	ខាងលិច
wet	dtor-dteuk; sarm	ទឹក; សើម
what?	a-way; ay	អ្វី; អី
when?	bpayl naa?	ពេលណា?
where?	ai-naa *or* ee-naa	ឯណា?
which	dail	ដែល
while, during	g'nong bpayl	ក្នុងពេល
white	bpoa-a sor	ពណ៌ស
who?	nay-uk naa; nor naa	អ្នកណា?; នរណា?
whole	dtay-ung mool; dtayng oh	ទាំងមូល; ទាំងអស់
why?	hait ay?	ហេតុអ្វី?
wide	dtoo-lee-ay	ទូលាយ
wife	bpra-bpoo-un	ប្រពន្ធ
will, shall	neung	នឹង
win	ch'nay-ah	ឈ្នះ
wind, breeze	k'yol	ខ្យល់
window	bong-oo-ich	បង្អួច
wipe	joot	ជូត
with	neung; ji-moo-ay	នឹង; ជាមួយ
woman	s'ray	ស្រី
wood (material)	cher	ឈើ
word	bpee-uk	ពាក្យ
work (n)	gaa ngee-a	ការងា
work (v)	t'wer gaa	ធ្វើការ
worry, be concerned	bproo-ay	ព្រួយ
write	sor-say	សរសេរ
wrong	koh	ខុស

xylophone	**ra-nee-ut**	រនៀត
year	**ch'num**	ឆ្នាំ
yell	**s'raik**	ស្រែក
yellow	**bpoa-a leu-ung**	ពណ៌លឿង
yes (male speaker)	**baat**	ប្រាទ
yes (female speaker)	**jaa**	ចាំ
yesterday	**m'serl meuñ**	ម្សិលមិញ
... yet?	**... reu nou?**	... ឬនៅ?
younger brother	**bpa-oan bproh**	ប្អូនប្រុស
younger sister	**bpa-oan s'ray**	ប្អូនស្រី
zero	**soan**	សូន្យ
zoo	**soo-un sut**	សួនសត្វ

Cambodian–English glossary

a-nOOñ-nyaat	to give permission	អនុញ្ញាត
aa-dteut	week	អាតិត្យ
aa-haa	food	អាហារ
aa-yOO	age; to be . . . years old	អាយុ
ai . . . weuñ	as for . . .	ឯ...វិញ
ai-naa/ee-naa?	where?	ឯណា
aing	you; self	ឯង
ao-ee	to give; cause; for	ឲ្យ
ay/a-way	what?	អ្វី
ay-lou nih	now	ឥឡូវនេះ
baa-rung	French	ប្រាំង
baan	to be able to, can	បាន
baang-gork	Bangkok	បាងកក
baat	yes (male)	ប្រាទ
bai	rice (cooked); food	បាយ
bai chaa	fried rice	បាយឆា
bar	if	បើ
bar un-jeung	in that case	បើអញ្ចឹង
bark	to open	បើក
b'day	husband	ប្តី

bee-a	beer	ពៀរ
beut	to close	បិទ
bom-norng	intention	បំណង
bom-rong	to intend	បំរុង
bon-dteuch bon-dtoo-ich	a little	បន្តិចបន្តួច
bon-dtor	to continue	បន្ត
bon-dtOOp	room	បន្ទប់
bon-dtOOp dayk	bedroom	បន្ទប់ដេក
bon-dtOOp dtor-dtoo-ul p'nyee-o	living room	បន្ទប់ទទួលភ្ញៀវ
bon-dtOOp ngoot dteuk	bathroom	បន្ទប់ងូតទឹក
bon-lai	vegetable	បន្លែ
bong	to lose	បង់
bong-aim	dessert, sweet (n)	បង្អែម
bong-gee-a	shrimp	បង្គារ
bong-goo-un	toilet	បង្គន់
bong-gorng	prawn	បង្គង
bong-kom	to force	បង្ខំ
bong-ree-un	to teach	បង្រៀន
borng bpa-oan	brothers and sisters	បងប្អូន
borng bproh	older brother	បងប្រុស
borng s'ray	older sister	បងស្រី
bot	to turn	បត់
bpa	to touch	ប៉ះ
bpa-oan bproh	younger brother	ប្អូនប្រុស
bpa-oan s'ray	younger sister	ប្អូនស្រី

bpairt	doctor	ពេទ្យ
... bpayk	too ...	... ពេក
bpayl	period of time; when	ពេល
bpay-uk gon-daal	middle	ពាក់កណ្ដាល
bpee	from	ពី
bpee	two	ពីរ
bpee bay	two or three; a few	ពីរ បី
bpee-uk	word	ពាក្យ
bpeuñ jeut	to be pleased	ពេញចិត្ត
bpeut mairn	actually	ពិតមែន
bpi-baak	difficult	ពិបាក
bpi-saa	to eat (polite)	ពិសារ
bpoa-ul	to touch	ពាល់
bpon-dtai	but	ប៉ុន្តែ
bpon-dteuch	a little	បន្តិច
bpon-maan?	how many?	ប៉ុន្មាន?
bpon-noh	only	ប៉ុណ្ណោះ
bpoo	waiter; uncle	ពូ
bpoo-gai	good at, clever	ពូកែ
bpoo-uk	group	ពូក
bpoo-uk-maak	friend	ពូកម៉ាក
bpol bpot	Pol Pot	ប៉ុល ពត
bpra-bpoo-un	wife	ប្រពន្ធ
bpra-dtair-ah	to meet, come across	ប្រទះ
bpra-dtayh	country	ប្រទេស
bpra-hail	approximately; perhaps	ប្រហែល
bpra-jee-a-joo-un	people	ប្រជាជន
bpra-yut	watch out!	ប្រយ័ត្ន

bpraa-saat	temple, fortress, ruins	ប្រាសាទ
bprai-sa-nee-ya-taan	post office	ប្រៃសណីយដ្ឋាន
bpray-ee	forest, jungle	ព្រៃ
bpreuk	morning	ព្រឹក
bproo-ah	because	ព្រោះ
bpruk	money	ប្រាក់
bpruk kai	salary	ប្រាក់ខែ
bprum	five	ប្រាំ
bprup	to inform, tell	ប្រាប់
brar	to use	ប្រើ
buñ-haa	problem	បញ្ហា
but	to lose, disappear	បាត់

chaa	to fry	ឆា
cha-ait	full (of food)	ឆ្អែត
ch'bah	clear, clearly	ច្បាស់
ch'lar-ee	to reply	ឆ្លើយ
ch'lorng	to cross	ឆ្លង
ch'moo-ah	to be named; name	ឈ្មោះ
ch'moo-ah dtra-goal	family name	ឈ្មោះត្រកូល
ch'ngai	far	ឆ្ងាយ
ch'nguñ	tasty	ឆ្ងាញ់
ch'num	year	ឆ្នាំ
ch'nung	cooking pot	ឆ្នាំង
ch'rook	pig, pork	ជ្រូក
chOOp	to stop	ឈប់
chun	to eat (used with monks)	ឆាន់
ch'wayng	left	ឆ្វេង

dai	hand	ដៃ
dail	which, where, who	ដែល
dail	used to	ដែល
dao-ee	by	ដោយ
dar	to walk; to work (machines)	ដើរ
darm	beginning	ដើម
darm-bay	in order to	ដើម្បី
day	land	ដី
deuk	to lead	ដឹក
deung	to know (facts)	ដឹង
deuñ	to chase away	ដេញ
doa	to exchange	ដូរ
doach	like, as	ដូច
doach-a-neh	so, therefore	ដូច្នេះ
doh s'rai	to solve (a problem)	ដោះស្រាយ
dol	to reach	ដល់
dom-nar	journey	ដំណើរ
dom-num	plant (n)	ដំណាំ
dong-hul	fan (electric)	ដង្ហាល់
dorng	edge	ដង
dorp	bottle	ដប
dtaa-raang m'hoap	menu	តារាងម្ហូប
dtaam	by; according to; to follow	តាម
dtai	but; only	តែ
dtai ... dtay	only	តែ ... ទេ
dtaim	stamp	តែមប្រិ៍

dtaing	always	តែង
. . . dtay?	*question word*	. . . ទេ?
dtay-sa-jor	tourism	ទេសចរណ៍
dtay-ung	all	ទាំង
dtay-ung bpee	both	ទាំងពីរ
dtee moo-ay	first	ទីមួយ
dtee bpee	second	ទីពីរ
dtee-a-hee-un	soldier	ទាហាន
dtee-ung	to be sure	ទៀង
dtee-ut	extra, further	ទៀត
dterp	then	ទើប
dteuh	direction	ទិស
dteuk	water, drink (n)	ទឹក
dteuk gork	ice	ទឹកកក
dteuk sot	drinking water	ទឹកសុទ្ធ
dteuñ	to buy	ទិញ
dtom-lay-uk	to drop	ទម្លាក់
dtoo-un-lay	river	ទន្លេ
dtor t'lai	to bargain	តថ្លៃ
dtor waa	to protest, complain	តវ៉ា
dtor-dtoo-ul	to receive	ទទួល
dtou	to go	ទៅ
dtou layng	to visit	ទៅលេង
dtra-jay-uk	cool, cold	ត្រជាក់
dtra-lop . . . weuñ	to return	ត្រឡប់ . . . វិញ
dtray	fish	ត្រី
dtrayk-or	pleased, delighted	ត្រេកអរ
dtrong	straight	ត្រង់

dtrong neung	right here	ត្រង់ហ្នឹង
dtrou	have to, must	ត្រូវ
dtrou	*passive marker*	ត្រូវ
dtung bpee	since	តាំងពី
dt'wee-a	door	ទ្វារ

ee-naa/ai-naa?	where?	ឯណា

foong	crowd, flock	ហ្វូង

ga-bul hoh	aeroplane	កប៉ាល់ហោះ
ga-bul dteuk	ship	កប៉ាល់ទឹក
gaa	to be married	ការ
gaa seuk-saa	education	ការសិក្សា
gaa-ri-yaa-lai	office	ការិយាល័យ
gart	to be born; to happen	កើត
gart	east	កើត
gay	he, she, they	គេ
g'dao	hot	ក្តៅ
geu	is; that is; namely	គឺ
geut	think, calculate	គិត
goa	cow, beef	គោ
goa-gaa goa-laa	Coca-Cola	កូកា-កូឡា
goa-ut	he, she, they	គាត់
goan	child	កូន
goan bproh	son	កូនប្រុស
goan s'ray	daughter	កូនស្រី
gom	don't	កុំ

gom-bpOOng	to be in the process of . . .	កំពុង
gon-lah	half	កន្លះ
gon-laing	place (n)	កន្លែង
goo-a	ought to, should	គួរ
goo-ee dtee-o	noodles	គុយទាវ
gor	then, so	ក៏
gor . . . dai	. . .too	ក៏ . . . ដែរ
gor saang	to build, construct	កសាង
gra-horm	red	ក្រហម
grao	outside	ក្រៅ
grao-ee	after	ក្រោយ
graom	under	ក្រោម
groa-ich	orange	ក្រូច
gror	poor	ក្រ
gun	to, toward	កាន់
gut	to cut	កាត់

hee-un	to dare to do something	ហ៊ាន
haang bai	restaurant	ហាងបាយ
hai-ee	already	ហើយ
hai-ee neung; neung	and	ហើយនឹង; នឹង
. . . hai-ee reu nou?	. . . yet (or not)?	ហើយឬនៅ?
hait	reason	ហេតុ
hao	to call, be called	ហៅ
hao m'hoap	to order food	ហៅម្ហូប
heul	hot, spicy	ហឹរ
hoap	to eat (used in rural areas)	ហូប

jaa	yes (female)	ចាំ
jaak	to depart	ចាក
jaam	Cham	ចាម
jaan	plate, dish	ចាន
jah	old	ចាស់
jai	to pay for	ចាយ
jaol	to throw away	ចោល
jee-a	is	ជា
. . . jee-a darm	. . . for example	. . . ជាដើម
jee-weut	life	ជីវិត
jeh	to know (a language)	ចេះ
jeh dtai . . .	to be always . . . (-ing)	ចេះតែ . . .
jerng	north	ជើង
jerng	foot	ជើង
jeu-a	to believe	ជឿ
jeun	China, Chinese	ចិន
jeuñ	to depart	ចេញ
jeuñ-jeum	to support	ចិញ្ចឹម
jeut la-or	kind	ចិត្តល្អ
joa	*imperative* (Do . . .)	ចូរ
joal	to enter	ចូល
joa-un	to step	ជាន់
joal-jeut	to like	ចូលចិត្ត
joh	. . . then; how about . . .?	ចុះ
joh t'lai	to lower the price	ចុះ ថ្លៃ
jom-gaa	farm, market garden	ចំការ
jom-nai	to spend	ចំណាយ
jom-ngai	distance	ចម្ងាយ

jom-noo-un	number, quantity	ចំនួន
jom-ngeu	disease	ជម្ងឺ
jong	to want to	ចង់
jop	to finish	ចប់
joo	sour	ជូរ
joon	to take, lead	ជូន
joo-ah jOOl	to repair	ជួសជុល
joo-ay	to help	ជួយ
joo-ul	to rent	ជួល
joo-un bor-ra-dtayh	foreigner	ជនបរទេស
joo-un jee-ut	nationality; people	ជនជាតិ
joo-un pee-ah kloo-un	refugee	ជនភៀសខ្លួន
joo-un gaal	sometimes	ជួនកាល
joo-up	to meet	ជួប
jOOm-ngeu	illness	ជម្ងឺ
jOOm-rOOm	(refugee) camp	ជំរំ
j'rarn	many	ច្រើន
j'rarn dtai	mostly . . .	ច្រើនតែ . . .
jum	to wait	ចាំ
jup	to begin	ចាប់
jup p'darm	to begin	ចាប់ផ្ដើម
jut	to assign, arrange	ចាត់
kaang	side	ខាង
kai	month	ខែ
kait	province	ខេត្ត
k'bai	near	ក្បែរ
k'daam	crab	ក្ដាម

kerñ	to see	យើញ
keung	angry	ខឹង
klah	some, somewhat	ខ្លះ
klee-un (bai)	to be hungry	ឃ្លាន(បាយ)
klee-un dteuk	to be thirsty	ឃ្លានទឹក
k'mai	Khmer, Cambodian	ខ្មែរ
k'mai gra-horm	Khmer Rouge	ខ្មែរក្រហម
k'mayng	child	ក្មេង
k'mee-un	not have, there aren't	គ្មាន
k'nong	in	ក្នុង
k'nyom	I	ខ្ញុំ
kOOm	town	ឃុំ
kroa-un bar	enough; quite well	គ្រាន់បើ
kroa-up baik	bomb	គ្រាប់បែក
kroo	teacher	គ្រូ
kroo-ah t'nuk	danger	គ្រោះថ្នាក់
krOOp	every	គ្រប់
krOOp-kroa-un	only	គ្រប់គ្រាន់
kreu-ung	utensil; tool	គ្រឿង
k'sot	destitute	ខ្សត់
kwah	to lack	ខ្វះ
la-or	well, good, beautiful	ល្អ
la-or jee-ung	better	ល្អជាង
l'bay	famous	ល្បី
lee-o	Lao	លាវ
lee-un	million	លាន
ler	on	លើ

leuch	west	លិច
l'morm	enough	ល្មម
l'ngee-ich	evening	ល្ងាច
loak	you (sing./plur.) (to address males)	លោក
loak s'ray	you (sing./plur.) (to address older females)	លោកស្រី
loo-ee	money	លុយ
loo-ich	to sneak (away); steal	លួច
loo-uk	to sell	លក់
lOOk loo-ee	to invade	លុកលុយ
lor merl	to try out	លមើល
leu	to hear	ឮ

maa-seen dtra-jay-uk	air-conditioner	ម៉ាស៊ីនត្រជាក់
ma-nOOh	person	មនុស្ស
mairn	indeed, really	មែន
mairn/mairn hai-ee	that's right!	មែនហើយ
mairn dtay?	isn't that so?	មែនទេ?
mairn reu?	really?	មែនឬ?
maong	hour	ម៉ោង
maych baan jee-a . . .?	why . . .?	ម៉េចបានជា. . .?
m'dai	mother	ម្ដាយ
m'dorng	one time	ម្ដង
mee	egg noodles	មី
meen	mine (explosive)	មីន
mee-un	to have; there is/are	មាន
merl	to look at	មើល

merl aan	to read	មើលអាន
meun ay dtay	never mind	មិនអ្វីទេ
meun . . . dtay	not	មិន . . . ទេ
meun . . .bpon-maan dtay	not very . . .	មិន. . .ប៉ុន្មានទេ
meun dtoa-un dtay	not yet	មិនទាន់ទេ
meun sou . . .	hardly, not very . . .	មិនសូវ
m'hoap	food	ម្ហូប
m'jah	owner	ម្ចាស់
m'nay-uk	*one person*	ម្នាក់
m'nee m'nee-a	to hurry	ម្នីម្នា
moak	come	មក
moak dol	to arrive	មកដល់
moa-un	chicken	មាន់
moo-ay	one	មួយ
mOOk	front; face	មុខ
mOOk-gaa	duty; job	មុខការ
mOOn	before	មុន
mOOn dom-boang	at first	មុនដំបូង
m'seul meuñ	yesterday	ម្សិលមិញ
nah	very	ណាស់
nai noa-um	to introduce	ណែនាំ
nay-uk	*classifier*	នាក់
nay-uk naa?	who?; anyone	អ្នកណា?
nay-uk poom	villager	អ្នកភូមិ
nay-uk s'rai	rice farmer	អ្នកវែស្រ
nay-uk s'rok	local people	អ្នកស្រុក

nee-a-dtee	minute	នាទី
nee-ung s'ray	you (sing./plur.) (to address younger females)	នាងស្រី
neuk s'rok	to miss home	នឹកស្រុក
neung	*future tense marker*; and	នឹង
ni-yee-ay	to speak	និយាយ
nih	this, this is	នេះ
nih-seut	student	និស្សិត
noa-um	to take, bring	នាំ
nou	to be situated at; to live at; at/in	នៅ
nOOh	that, that is	នោះ
n'yum	to eat	ញ៉ាំ

oa	*exclamation*	អូ
oa-bpOOk	father	ឪពុក
oa-bpOOk m'dai	parents	ឪពុកម្ដាយ
oh	completely	អស់
om-bpee	about, concerning	អំពី
ong-gaa	organisation	អង្គការ
ong-gor	husked rice	អង្ករ
ong-gul, bpee ong-gul	when?	អង្គាល់; ពីអង្គាល់
ong-klayh	English	អង់គ្លេស
or-gOOn	thank you	អរគុណ
ot klee-un	to starve	អត់ឃ្លាន

pa-aim	sweet (adj)	ផ្អែម
pain-gaa	plan	ផែនការ

p'dom k'nee-a	gathered together	ផ្ដុំគ្នា
pee-a-saa	language	ភាសា
pee-uk j'rarn	majority	ភាគច្រើន
pee-uk roy	percentage	ភាគរយ
plah	to move	ផ្លាស់
plai cher	fruit	ផ្លែឈើ
plairt	moment	ភ្លែត
plee-um	immediately	ភ្លាម
plee-ung	rain	ភ្លៀង
plou	road	ផ្លូវ
p'nOOm	hill; mountain	ភ្នំ
p'nOOm bpeuñ	Phnom Penh	ភ្នំពេញ
p'nyar	to send	ភ្ជើរ
p'nyee-o	guest	ភ្ញៀវ
poa-ja-nee-ya-taan	restaurant	ភោជនីយដ្ឋាន
poom	village	ភូមិ
poom-mi-pee-uk	region	ភូមិភាគ
poom-mi-saah	geography	ភូមិសាស្ត្រ
porng	too	ផង
p'saa oa-reu-say	O Russei Market	ផ្សារ អូឬស្សី
p'saa t'may	New Market	ផ្សារ ថ្មី
p'sayng	different	ផ្សេង
p'sayng p'sayng	various	ផ្សេង ៗ
p'dtay-ah	house	ផ្ទះ
ra-boh	of; thing	របស់
ra-boo-ah	to be wounded	របួស
ra-dou	season	រដូវ

ra-dou bprung	dry season	រដូវប្រាំង
ra-dou plee-ung	rainy season	រដូវភ្លៀង
ra-dou ra-ngee-a	cool season	រដូវរងា
ra-hoat	throughout	រហូត
ra-leeng	completely	រលីង
ra-see-ul	afternoon	រសៀល
ra-yair-a	period of time	រយៈ
ree-ul	riel (unit of currency)	រៀល
ree-un	to study, learn	រៀន
ree-up jum	to prepare	រៀបចាំ
ree-uch-a-tee-a-nee	capital city	រាជធានី
reu	or	ឬ
reu dtay?	*question form*	ឬទេ?
reu-ung	story	រឿង
roa-ul	every	រាល់
roo-ah jee-ut	taste, flavour	រសជាតិ
roo-ah nou	to live, dwell	រស់នៅ
roo-ich	then	រួច
roo-ut	to run	រត់
roop tort	photograph	រូបថត
rOOm-kaan	annoyed, disturbed	រខាន
rork	to look for	រក
rork see	to earn a living	រកស៊ី
sa-aat	beautiful; clean	ស្អាត
sa-aik	tomorrow	ស្អែក
sa-pee-up	state, condition	សភាព
saa	to repeat, do again	សា

saa-laa ree-un	school	សាលារៀន
saa-ra-moo-un-dtee	museum	សារមន្ទីរ
saam seup	thirty	សាមសិប
sai-ich	meat	សាច់
s'bee-ung	supplies, provisions	ស្បៀង
s'dum	right	ស្ដាំ
s'dup baan	to understand	ស្ដាប់បាន
s'dup meun baan dtay	to not understand	ស្ដាប់មិនបានទេ
see	to eat (used for animals)	ស៊ី
see-o pou	books	សៀវភៅ
seun	first	សិន
s'koa-ul	to know (people, places)	ស្គាល់
s'lup	to die	ស្លាប់
s'nuk	to stay (temporarily)	ស្នាក់
soam	please	សូម
soam-bay	even, including	សូម្បី
som	to ask for	សុំ
sok sop-bai jee-a dtay?	how are you?	សុខសប្បាយជាទេ?
som-bot	letter	សំបុត្រ
som-bpoo-ut	cloth; skirt	សំពត់
som-kun	important	សំខាន់
som-layng	voice; accent	សំឡេង
som-lee-uk bom-bpay-uk	clothes	សំលៀកបំពាក់
som-lor	soup, stew (n)	សម្ល
som-lor gor-goa	(Cambodian dish)	សម្លកកូរ
som-lor ma-joo	(Cambodian dish)	សម្លម្ជូ
som-lup	to kill	សម្លាប់

som-naang	luck	សំណាង
som-raak	to rest	សំរាក
som-raich jeut	to decide	សំរេចចិត្ត
som-rup	for	សំរាប់
son-leuk	classifier for stamps	សន្លឹក
son-dti-pee-up	peace	សន្តិភាព
son-taa-gee-a	Manorom Hotel	សណ្ឋាគារ
son-taa-gee-a ma-noa-rom	Manorom Hotel	សណ្ឋាគារមនោរម្យ
soo-a	to ask	សួរ
soo-a s'day	hello	សួស្ដី
soo-un	garden	សួន
sop t'ngai nih	nowadays	សព្វថ្ងៃនេះ
sor-say	to write	សរសេរ
sot	pure	សុទ្ធ
sot dtai	all, entirely	សុទ្ធតែ
s'rai	rice field	ស្រែ
s'rou	unhusked rice	ស្រូវ
s'rok	country; district	ស្រុក
s'roo-ul	easy; convenient	ស្រួល
s'rup dtai	suddenly	ស្រាប់តែ
staad oa-lum-bpeek	Olympic Stadium	ស្ថាតអូឡាំពិក
stair-ah	blocked up	ស្ទះ
ster dtai	almost	ស្ទើតែ
steut	to be situated	ស្ថិត
suñ-nyaa	sign	សញ្ញា
taa	to say	ថា

tai	Thai	ថៃ
tai ray-uk-saa	to care for	ថៃរក្សា
t'baañ	to weave	ត្បាញ
t'boang	south	ត្បូង
tee-ut aa-gaah	weather	ធាតុអាកាស
t'lai	expensive	ថ្លៃ
t'lai bpon-maan?	how much does it cost?	ថ្លៃប៉ុន្មាន?
t'lai ch'noo-ul	rent	ថ្លៃឈ្នួល
t'loa-up neung	accustomed to	ធ្លាប់នឹង
t'may	new	ថ្មី
t'nuk	class	ថ្នាក់
t'num bpairt	medicine	ថ្នាំពេទ្យ
t'ngai	day; sun	ថ្ងៃ
t'ngai aa-dteut	Sunday	ថ្ងៃអាទិត្យ
t'ngai bra-hoa-a	Thursday	ថ្ងៃព្រហស្បតិ៍
t'ngai bpOOt	Wednesday	ថ្ងៃពុធ
t'ngai jun	Monday	ថ្ងៃចន្ទ
t'ngai ong-gee-a	Tuesday	ថ្ងៃអង្គារ
t'ngai sao	Saturday	ថ្ងៃសៅរ៍
t'ngai sok	Friday	ថ្ងៃសុក្រ
t'ngai dtrong	noon	ថ្ងៃត្រង់
toa-um-ma-daa	usually	ធម្មតា
tom	big	ធំ
tor-nee-a-gee-a	bank	ធនាគារ
tort roop	to take a photo	ថតរូប
t'wer	to do, make	ធ្វើ
t'wer dom-nar	to travel	ធ្វើដំណើរ
t'wer gaa	to work	ធ្វើការ

t'wer s'rai	to do rice farming	ធ្វើស្រែ
uk-sor	letter (of the alphabet)	អក្សរ
uk-sor k'mai	Cambodian script	អក្សរខ្មែរ
uñ-jeuñ	*polite request form*	អញ្ជើញ
way-ung	palace	វាំង
wee-ul (s'rai)	(rice) plain	វាលស្រែ
weut-yaa-lai	college	វិទ្យាល័យ
wi-nee-a-dtee	second (n)	វិនាទី
woa-ut p'nOOm	Wat Phnom	វត្តភ្នំ
yaang	like	យ៉ាង
yerng	we, us	យើង
yerng k'nyom	we, us	យើងខ្ញុំ
yoak	to bring	យក
yoak jeut dtOOk duk	to be interested,	យកចិត្តទុកដាក់
	pay attention to	
yoo	a long time	យូរ
yoo-ul	to understand	យល់
yoo-un	Vietnamese	យួន
yOOp	night	យប់

Index

The references are to lesson numbers.